The Impact of the Minimum Wage on Regional Labor Markets

The Impact of
the Minimum Wage on
Regional Labor Markets

Ronald J. Krumm

American Enterprise Institute for Public Policy Research
Washington and London

Ronald J. Krumm is a research fellow at the University of Chicago.

I thank Gary Becker, Yale Brozen, Dennis Carlton, John P. Gould, Philip Graves, James Heckman, Sherwin Rosen, George Tolley, Arnold Zellner, and members of the workshop in econometrics, the econometrics and statistics colloquium, and the urban economics workshop at the University of Chicago for useful comments and suggestions. I also thank Wayne Miller and William Roule for their most capable research assistance. The usual disclaimer for remaining errors applies.

R.J.K.

Library of Congress Cataloging in Publication Data

Krumm, Ronald J
    The impact of the minimum wage on regional labor markets.

    (AEI studies ; 310)
    1. Wages—Minimum wage—United States. 2. Labor supply—United States. 3. Regional economics. I. Title. II. Title: Regional labor markets. III. Series: American Enterprise Institute for Public Policy Research. AEI studies ; 310.
HD4918.K78   331.12'0973   80–28263
ISBN 0–8447–3425–X
ISBN 0–8447–3426–8 (pbk.)

AEI Studies 310

Printed in the United States of America

Contents

1 INTRODUCTION AND OVERVIEW   1

2 LEGISLATIVE BACKGROUND   6

    Federal Minimum-Wage Legislation   7
    Trends in Federal Coverage and Minimum-Wage
      Level   12
    State Minimum-Wage Legislation   18
    Combined State and Federal Legislation   19
    Summary   21

3 FRAMEWORK   22

    Labor Market Conditions   22
    Skill Differences among Workers   24
    Partial Coverage: The Early Years   27
    Complete Coverage: The Trend   29
    Output Market Impacts   35
    Nonwage Forms of Payment and On-the-Job
      Training   36
    Summary   38

4 MINIMUM-WAGE IMPACTS IN A DIVERSE SPATIAL ECONOMY   40

    An Overview of Location of People and Jobs   41
    The Impacts of Minimum Wages   42
    Summary   52

5   EMPIRICAL FINDINGS   53

     Implications for Empirical Modeling   53
     Empirical Modeling and Results   54
     Summary   58

6   SUMMARY AND POLICY IMPLICATIONS   61

APPENDIXES   63
     Appendix A. A General Approach for Examining
      Impacts of Minimum Wages   63
     Appendix B. Empirical Modeling and Results   80

LIST OF TABLES
     1. Estimated Proportion of Nonsupervisory
        Employees Covered by the Basic Minimum
        Wage and by the Rate Applicable to Newly
        Covered Workers, by Industry,
        1947–1978   13
     2. Federal Minimum-Wage Levels and Estimated
        Numbers of Employees Covered by the
        FLSA   15
     3. Employees Covered by Federal and State
        Minimum-Wage Legislation as of February 1,
        1970   20
     4. Manufacturing Employment, by Region, 1963
        and 1977   43
     5. Net Migration of the Population, by Region,
        1960–1970   44
     6. Percentage Change in the Average Wage Due
        to a 1 Percent Change in the National
        Minimum Wage, by Industry   55
     7. Effects of Regional Deflators on the Magnitude
        of Percentage Change in Average Wages Due
        to a 1 Percent Change in the National
        Minimum Wage, by Industry   57
     8. Percentage Change in Average Wages in an
        SMSA as a Result of an Increase in the
        Percentage of Employment Covered by
        Minimum-Wage Legislation, by Industry   59
     9. Pooled Cross Section of Time Series Classical
        Least Squares Estimates of Equation 28, by

Industry (time dummy variables not
included)   86

10. Effects of Changes in Minimum Wages and
    Coverage on Average Real Wages, by
    Industry (time-specific effects not
    included)   88

11. Pooled Cross Section of Time Series Classical
    Least Squares Estimates of Equation 28, by
    Industry (time dummy variables
    included)   90

12. Effects of Changes in Minimum Wages and
    Coverage on Average Real Wages, by
    Industry (time-specific effects included)   92

LIST OF FIGURES

1. Percentage of Employment Covered by Federal
   Minimum-Wage Legislation, by Industry,
   1960–1977   14

2. Basic Federal Minimum Wage Deflated by U.S.
   Consumer Price Index, 1941–1978   17

3. Basic Federal Minimum Wage Deflated by
   Average Hourly Wage in Manufacturing,
   1941–1977   18

4. Supply and Demand of Worker Skills   24

5. Distribution of Workers by Skill Level   25

6. Distribution of Workers by Wage   26

7. Effect of a Minimum Wage on Wages and
   Employment in Covered and Uncovered
   Industries: The Case of No Worker Wage
   Effects   28

8. Effect of a Minimum Wage on Wages and
   Employment in a Fully Covered Economy:
   The Case of a Fixed Labor Force   30

9. Supply and Demand Determination of
   Employment and Price of a Unit of Skill in
   the Presence of a Minimum Wage: The Case
   of a Fixed Labor Force   31

10. Supply and Demand Determination of
    Employment and Price of a Unit of Skill in
    the Presence of a Minimum Wage: The Case
    of a Nonfixed Labor Force   34

11. Effect of a Minimum Wage on Wages When
    the Ripple Effect Induces Entry of New

Workers into the Labor Market   35

12. Effect of a Minimum Wage on Wages and Employment in the Presence of On-the-Job Training   38

13. Effect of a National Minimum Wage on Wages and Employment in High- and Low-Cost-of-Living Regions: The Ripple Effect without Flows of Workers between Regions   46

14. Supply and Demand of Worker Skills, Determination of Price per Unit of Skill, and Skills Employed for a National Minimum Wage Applied Uniformly in High- and Low-Cost-of-Living Regions: No Worker Flows between Regions   48

15. Effect of a National Minimum Wage on Wages and Employment in High- and Low-Cost-of-Living Regions: Flows of Workers between Regions   49

16. Effect of Changes in a National Minimum Wage in High- and Low-Cost-of-Living Regions   51

17. Distribution of Worker Skills in Conjunction with a Minimum Wage   65

18. Determination of Price per Unit of Skill and Total Skills Employed from Demand and Supply of Worker Skills in an Economy with and without a Minimum Wage   66

19. Effect of a Minimum Wage Applied in Only One Industry That in the Absence of a Minimum Wage Employs Only Some of the Total Skills in the Economy   72

20. Effect of a National Minimum Wage in the Presence of Equilibrium Cost-of-Living Differences among Regions   76

1

Introduction and Overview

Federal minimum-wage legislation in the United States was initiated within the Fair Labor Standards Act (FLSA) of 1938, with minimum-wage concerns only part of a more comprehensive policy involving federal regulation of working conditions. The purpose of this act was to correct alleged impairment to interstate economic activity resulting from and exacerbating unacceptable labor conditions, as stated in the FLSA of 1938:

> SEC. 2 (a) The Congress hereby finds that the existence in industries engaged in commerce or in the production of goods for commerce, of labor conditions detrimental to the maintenance of the minimum standard of living necessary for health, efficiency and general well-being of workers (1) causes commerce and the channels and instrumentalities of commerce to be used to spread and perpetuate such labor conditions among the workers of the several states; (2) burdens commerce and the free flow of goods in commerce; (3) constitutes an unfair method of competition in commerce; (4) leads to labor disputes burdening and obstructing commerce and the free flow of goods in commerce and (5) interferes with the orderly and fair marketing of goods in commerce.

This act (and subsequent amendments) had as its goal to "correct and as rapidly as practicable to eliminate the conditions above referred to in such industry without substantially curtailing employment or earning power." Policies initiated for this purpose included minimum-wage constraints, maximum hour/overtime regulations, and child labor provisions. Amendments to the act have served to increase the extent of federal intervention in these areas, as well as the magnitudes of the limits set.

We need first to examine the extent to which federal policies in particular have served to mitigate the labor conditions postulated by the FLSA of 1938 to result in harmful effects on commerce, and we must also determine if any effects of the legislation have spread to labor conditions among the states. In this regard, the postulated causal relationship between labor conditions and their impact on interstate commerce is not an issue. Rather, the focus is on the extent to which the policy remedies under this legislation enhance labor conditions. If they have little effect, the legislation itself, even in light of its assumptions, is misguided and inappropriate.

A second and complementary task is to determine the extent to which minimum wages and the associated policy instruments serve to improve the conditions of commerce and the free flow of goods in commerce. Again, if they have little effect, the legislation is inappropriate and misguided.

This monograph investigates the issues involved in federal minimum-wage standards in the context of a diverse spatial economy, where the characteristics of production and labor-market conditions vary across space. Such an approach is especially relevant for analyzing the effects of minimum-wage legislation in the United States, where economic activity is spread among many distinct areas. The U.S. minimum wage is applied nonuniformly to employment in different industries, although the trend has been toward complete coverage of employment in all facets of life. The national minimum wage is applied uniformly in covered industries among regions; however, differences in cost of living and amenities (for example, mild climate) among regions lead to differences in the real minimum-wage level associated with a uniform national minimum wage.

Chapter 2 presents an overview of federal minimum-wage legislation in the United States, beginning with the FLSA of 1938. Amendments to this act have increased the coverage of employment subject to the minimum and changed the level of the minimum itself. The general pattern has been for the real minimum wage to increase because of legislated increases in the nominal minimum wage, with inflation offsetting the increases to some extent. In addition to federal minimum-wage restrictions, individual states have had minimum-wage standards that increase coverage of employment under minimum-wage legislation. In most cases state minimum wages are less than the amount set by the FLSA, with the federal minimum applying to those workers jointly covered by state and federal law. Coverage by federal legislation is incomplete, however, and the state minimum wage applies to those cases not covered by federal provisions.

Chapter 3 presents a framework for analyzing the impacts of a minimum wage in a single, nonspatial economy. The demand for labor services is the sum of demands in all industry categories and depends on the price of labor services. The supply of labor services depends on both the number of laborers and the skill level of each laborer. Skill differences among workers lead to wage differences in the absence of a minimum wage because workers of different skills provide different levels of labor services in production. Because workers can flow between industries, the price of a unit of skill is determined by total industry demand and the economywide supply of labor skills.

Introduction of a minimum wage that applies to employment in some industries leads to flows of workers among covered and uncovered sectors. The minimum wage means that workers previously earning less in the covered sector either must have increased wages or must not be employed there. Employers have little incentive to increase the wages of these lower-skill workers because they can replace the services of the low-skill workers with higher-skill workers previously employed in uncovered industries. The result is that the low-skill workers flow to the uncovered sector, their labor services replaced by high-skill workers who flow into the covered sector from the uncovered sector. While artificially segmenting employment of workers possessing different skills, a minimum wage applied only to a sector of the economy that is small enough has no net impact on employment or compensation of either high- or low-skill workers. Moreover, under such conditions there is no change in the costs of labor services in the economy and hence no impact of the minimum wage on product markets. Increased coverage or a high enough minimum wage results in a breakdown of replacement flows of workers of different skills.

In a fully covered economy, or when replacement flows of workers are not possible, the imposition of a minimum wage unambiguously worsens the conditions of low-skill workers, while those who gain are high-skill workers. Low-skill workers are disemployed (in the case of almost full coverage, some remain employed, but at lower wages), while higher-skill workers receive higher wages. The minimum wage reduces the supply of skills that are employable in the economy and hence increases the value of those workers with skill levels high enough to be employed. The magnitudes of employment loss (low-skill workers) and compensation gains to those remaining employed (high-skill workers) are directly related to the increase in the price per unit of skill induced by the minimum wage, which is commonly referred to as the "ripple effect." Increased labor-force participation of higher-skill workers induced by increased labor mar-

3

ket compensation results in greater disemployment of lower-skill workers and smaller increases in labor costs.

Chapter 4 extends the framework developed in chapter 3 to a diverse spatial economy. Just as flows of workers of different skills among covered and uncovered industries in a nonspatial economy allow for a lessened impact of a minimum wage on worker employment and compensation patterns, flows of people among regions allow for the reduction of adverse impacts of uneven coverage among areas. State minimum-wage legislation and the uneven coverage of industries by federal legislation mean that employment will be covered to a greater extent in some states than in others. Replacement flows of workers of different skills among states in the presence of uneven coverage lead to results similar to those for partial coverage in a nonspatial economy.

Variation in costs of purchasing local goods and services, as well as in location-specific amenities (such as a pleasant climate), can lead to differences among areas in nominal wage levels for a particular worker. A worker living in a high-cost-of-living area earning a higher wage may be just as well off as another worker living in a low-cost-of-living area with a lower wage. The national minimum wage is applied uniformly among areas that differ in cost of living and amenities. Hence a worker who could earn four dollars an hour in New York City and two dollars an hour in Sun City (and be just as well off) would be directly affected by a national minimum wage of three dollars if he were living in Sun City, while he would not be directly affected if he were living in New York City. In essence, a uniform national minimum wage corresponds to a higher real minimum in low-cost-of-living, high-amenity areas and a lower real minimum in high-cost-of-living, low-amenity areas.

In the presence of uneven real-minimum-wage restrictions among areas, flows of workers can lead to lessened impacts of the uniform national minimum wage on employment opportunities of low-skill workers and their resulting compensation. Workers with skills that would earn less than the minimum wage in otherwise low-nominal-wage areas but would earn more than the minimum in otherwise high-nominal-wage areas will flow to the high-nominal-wage areas. High-skill workers, on the other hand, will flow to low-nominal-wage areas, partially replacing the services previously performed by the lower-skill workers. An important result of such flows induced by the national minimum wage is the concentration of lower-skill workers in many of the central cities of the United States, usually characterized by high costs of living. Further increases in the national minimum wage lead to the disemployment of these workers, with welfare burdens falling on central city governments currently facing fiscal strain.

Chapter 5 presents empirical findings indicating that increases in the national minimum wage do indeed lead to flows of the lower-skill workers to high-cost-of-living areas. Further, increased coverage of employment in an area due to either state or federal minimum-wage legislation leads to a decrease in the average wage in previously covered industries. The implications of this finding are that the ripple effect induces labor-force participation of medium-skill workers, who replace low-skill workers in the economy. Increased coverage has tended to decrease the employment opportunities of low-skill workers, while the increased labor-force participation of medium-skill workers has lessened the impact of increased coverage on labor costs.

Federal minimum-wage legislation is based on the idea that conditions that lead some workers to earn low wages are spread by interstate commerce and indeed interfere with the free flow of commerce among areas and that minimum wages are a means by which these labor market conditions can be remedied. This work suggests that minimum-wage legislation, and not commerce, impairs the employment and compensation opportunities of low-skill workers. Further, it is the minimum wage that spreads and exacerbates conditions "detrimental to the maintenance of the minimum standard of living" among the states.

2

Legislative Background

Federal minimum-wage legislation, starting with the Fair Labor Standards Act of 1938 and expanded through subsequent amendments, has greatly increased federal regulation of labor market conditions and associated economic activity. The direct constraint is on characteristics of employment in industries covered by the legislation. The extent to which federal regulation interferes with employment decisions and conditions of work has increased substantially, not only because of increases in the level of the federal minimum wage but also because amendments to the FLSA of 1938 have expanded coverage. A prominent concern of this monograph is to examine the implications of the increased application of this legislation to more and more economic activities, together with changes in the level of the minimum wage itself.

In conjunction with federal minimum-wage legislation, which presupposes that labor market conditions have potential interstate ramifications, many states have adopted minimum-wage legislation of their own. State minimum wages apply to those employees and employers not covered by federal minimum-wage regulations. While the federal minimum-wage level is applied uniformly to workers covered under federal legislation, regardless of location, state minimum-wage levels and coverage conditions have varied markedly among states at any point in time and have often changed at times different from those for the federal minimum. Interaction among state and federal minimum-wage regulations suggests that effects of changes in the federal legislation will differ among regions, depending on state-specific legislation.

This chapter presents a short legislative history of federal and state minimum-wage legislation, providing a background for more complete examination of its effects on economic activity and labor

6

market conditions. Measurement of the changing nature of federal coverage and the associated minimum wage is discussed and integrated with state-specific legislative considerations.

Federal Minimum-Wage Legislation

The FLSA of 1938 initiated federal authority on a substantial scale to regulate wages and other characteristics of employment. This act established policies concerning minimum wages, hours worked, and child labor, as well as a variety of exemptions based on type of employer and type of employee, in an attempt to improve employment conditions for low-wage, low-skill workers and to enhance the free flow of commerce among states. The focus of this legislative summary is on minimum-wage levels and the extent of application of constraints (coverage) established by the FLSA of 1938 and subsequent amendments, with only minor attention given to the other aspects of the legislation.

Fair Labor Standards Act of 1938. The FLSA of 1938 established minimum wages for all employees engaged in commerce or in the production of goods for commerce. Commerce was defined as "trade, commerce, transportation, or communication among the several states or from any state to any place outside thereof," with the legislation apparently applying only to economic activity that involved interstate trade.

Employers (notably excluding government employees at local, state, and federal levels) were required to pay each employee engaged in commerce or in the production of goods for commerce at a rate not less than $0.25 per hour for the following year, increasing to $0.30 per hour in the following six years, and finally reaching $0.40 per hour after that time. These gradual increases were meant to allow for adjustment to the new legislation so that the employment and earning power of affected workers would not be substantially curtailed.

Overtime hour wage restrictions were introduced requiring payment of not less than one and one-half the regular hourly wage to employees for any hours over forty hours per week. Partial exemptions to the overtime hour wage restrictions were provided for some labor contracts made under collective bargaining arrangements, in some seasonal industries, and in a few industry-specific cases.

A variety of exemptions to the minimum-hourly-wage and hours-worked provisions of the FLSA of 1938 were included in the legislation, some based on characteristics of the employer and others on characteristics of the employee. Exemptions were made for executive, administrative, and professional positions, as well as for those engaged in local retailing capacities and those employed as outside salesmen. Employees of retail or service industries, the greater part of whose business was intrastate, were exempted from the minimum-wage and hours-worked provisions, as were various employees in transportation industries. Agricultural employees were wholly exempt from these provisions. Exemptions such as these essentially imposed the brunt of the legislation on employees in mining and manufacturing sectors of the economy, with those in wholesale trade, contract construction, and transportation and public utilities covered somewhat less.

While the exemptions above related mostly to the type of economic activity (industry) in which a worker was employed, a further set of exemptions was provided for learners, apprentices, messengers, and handicapped workers (whose conditions of employment were subject to the discretion of the administrator) in recognition of the potential decreases in employment opportunities for these types of workers stemming from the legislated wage floor.

Amendments to the FLSA of 1938 in 1949 and 1955 served to increase the level of the minimum wage to $0.75 per hour starting in January 1945 and to $1.00 in March 1956. Other provisions were made in these legislative actions, further complicating the hours-worked regulations though not substantially altering the extent to which the legislation covered other industries or types of workers.

Fair Labor Standards Amendments of 1961. The first substantial changes in the content of the FLSA of 1938 resulted from the 1961 amendments. In addition to increases in the level of the minimum wage applicable to those already covered by previous legislation, expansion of coverage was initiated.

Included in expanded coverage were those employed in an enterprise engaged in commerce or the production of goods for commerce, enterprises being "the related activities performed (either through unified operation or common control) by any person or persons for a common business purpose, and [including] . . . all such activities whether performed in one or more establishments or by one or more corporate or other organizational units." This clause essentially changed the scope of coverage from the establishment itself to those larger organizations of which the establishment was only a part. Enterprises engaged in commerce or in the production of goods and services for commerce were specified to include:

1. enterprises with one or more retail or service establishments with annual gross volume of sales of the enterprise over $1 million if the enterprise engaged in interstate activities with annual volume over $250,000
2. certain transportation industries with annual gross volume of sales greater than $1 million
3. any establishment of an enterprise with employees engaged in commerce or in the production of goods for commerce if the annual gross volume of sales of the enterprise was greater than $1 million
4. enterprises engaged in construction or reconstruction activities with gross volume of sales greater than $350,000
5. gasoline service establishments with gross volume of sales greater than $250,000

The inclusion of enterprises as described above under federal minimum-wage coverage substantially increased the number of employees covered in industries with previously low coverage. Moreover, determination of coverage from size of sales meant that a distinction was based on size of economic activity, even though the same economic function was carried out by various firms within an industry.

Exemptions were greatly modified by the 1961 amendments, which included a variety of industry-specific coverage provisions. Employees of a retail or service establishment employed in executive or administrative positions were subject to coverage if fewer than 40 percent of their hours were in that capacity. Exemptions for employees in retail or service establishments (the greater part of whose sales were made within the state) were retained if they were not part of an enterprise or if they were part of an enterprise but their gross annual volume of sales was less than $250,000. Moreover, employees of hotels, motels, restaurants, motion picture theaters, some seasonal service establishments, and hospitals and similar institutions were exempt even if they were part of an enterprise.

Restrictions on coverage were determined in some cases by the purchaser of services, with employees in establishments dealing in laundering, cleaning, or repairing clothing or fabrics (if more than 50 percent of annual volume of sales was interstate) exempt only if 75 percent of the establishment's annual dollar volume of sales of those services was not made to customers engaged in mining, manufacturing, transportation, or communication business.

Retail and service establishments fitting the exemptions above were not covered if those goods were made or processed at the establishment and if more than 85 percent of the annual volume of sales of such goods was made within the state. Exemptions based on worker characteristics were extended to full-time students outside their school hours in retail and service establishments, provided the job was not ordinarily performed by a full-time employee.

Inclusion of enterprises increased the extent of coverage substantially, the number of covered workers engaged in contract construction increasing by 80 percent, those in retail trade increasing by more than 1,000 percent, and those in transportation and public utilities increasing by approximately 8 percent.

The basic minimum wage for those covered before the 1961 amendments was increased to $1.15 from September 1961 through August 1963 and to $1.25 thereafter. For those newly covered by the 1961 amendments, the minimum was set at $1.00 from September 1961 through August 1964. It increased to $1.15 the following year and to $1.25 thereafter, bringing the minimum wage applicable to newly covered workers equal to that for workers previously covered and keeping in step with gradual extensions of the imposition of federal minimum-wage constraints.

Fair Labor Standards Amendments of 1966. Major revisions of the minimum-wage provisions of the FLSA of 1938 and previous amendments were initiated in the 1966 amendments, setting the stage for even more extreme extensions legislated in later years. In conjunction with increases in the level of the minimum wage, these revisions greatly increased the scope and magnitude of coverage under federal minimum-wage legislation.

A covered enterprise engaged in commerce or in the production of goods for commerce was, from February 1967 through January 1969, one that had an annual volume of sales greater than $500,000 or, if it was a gasoline service establishment, a gross volume of sales greater than $250,000; starting in February 1969 the enterprise was one with gross volume of sales greater than $250,000. These reductions in the size of business (as indicated by annual volume of sales) subject to coverage by the federal minimum-wage restrictions were exacerbated by the general increase in nominal prices over the period, the consumer price index increasing more than 20 percent between 1962 and 1969. Further, enterprises engaged in laundering, cleaning, or repairing clothing, or in construction or reconstruction, as well as hospitals and other, similar institutions and schools, were included as enterprises.

Exemptions for retail and service establishments that were not part of enterprises retained the same nominal annual-volume-of-sales

10

restriction, although such exemptions for laundry and dry cleaning concerns were repealed.

Coverage was extended to agricultural employees by the 1966 amendments, although some types of workers were still exempt in this industry. The exemptions for various industry categories were further complicated because of these amendments.

The basic minimum wage applicable to all those previously covered by federal minimum-wage legislation (including those newly covered by the 1961 amendments) was increased to $1.40 from February 1967 through January 1968 and to $1.60 thereafter. The rate applicable to newly covered nonfarm employees was set at $1.00 per hour starting February 1967 and extending through January 1968 and increased $0.15 per hour each year thereafter until February 1971, at which time the rate of $1.60 was attained, bringing parity with those previously covered. Newly covered farm workers were to be paid not less than $1.00 per hour the first year of enactment, increasing to $1.15 the second year and to $1.30 thereafter.

Fair Labor Standards Amendments of 1974. The 1974 amendments for the first time brought state and federal government employees under coverage. Moreover, domestic service workers received coverage, with an amendment to the preamble of the FLSA stating "that Congress further finds that the employment of persons in domestic service in households affects commerce."

In addition to the extension of government wage restrictions to these two new employment categories, the sales volume exemption applicable to retail and service establishments was decreased to $225,000 starting in January 1975, declined to $200,000 starting in January 1976, and was dropped altogether as a provision starting in January 1977.

Partial exemptions for full-time students in retail and service establishments were greatly complicated as a result of the 1974 amendments, most likely very much reducing incentives for employers to take advantage of exemptions of this type.

The minimum wage applicable to those employees covered before the 1966 amendments rose to $2.00 per hour from May 1974 through December 1974, increased to $2.10 in 1975, and climbed to $2.30 thereafter. The rate for newly covered workers was set at $1.90 until the end of 1974 and grew each year thereafter until 1977, at which time parity was reached with the minimum-wage level for those covered before the 1974 amendments. The minimum applicable to agricultural employees was set at $1.60 until the end of 1974 and increased by $0.20 every year thereafter through 1976. It was set at parity with the minimum for other covered employees, or $2.30, from 1977 on.

Fair Labor Standards Amendments of 1977. Further modifications of exemptions and increased levels of the minimum wage were legislated in the 1977 amendments. Increases in the minimum brought it to $2.65 in 1978, to $2.90 in 1979, and to $3.05 starting in 1980. It will rise to $3.35 in 1981.

The definition of a covered enterprise was modified to include an enterprise composed exclusively of one or more retail or service establishments with annual volume of sales not less than $259,000 beginning in July 1978, increasing to $275,000 in July 1979, to $325,000 in July 1980, and to $365,000 after December 1981. Some simplifications for students' employment by small business was provided, although no substantial changes in the provisions for student employment were made.

Trends in Federal Coverage and Minimum-Wage Level

Table 1 presents a summary of the extent of coverage, according to industry category, of the federal minimum wage. While mining and manufacturing sectors have been covered very fully since the inception of the legislation, the various amendments discussed above have served to alter the extent of coverage in other sectors of the U.S. economy very much, with recent adjustments making most of the industry groups almost fully covered. Combining newly covered workers at the applicable minimum-wage level and workers covered by the basic minimum wage, figure 1 presents an index of the percentage of workers covered by federal minimum-wage legislation arranged by industry group. This index weights newly covered workers by the ratio of the minimum wage for newly covered workers to the basic minimum wage. Sharp increases in coverage due to an amendment increase the index gradually as the minimum wage applicable to newly covered workers increases to match the basic minimum. Table 2 summarizes changes in the level of the federal minimum wage due to the various amendments since 1938. If we are to capture the true magnitude of this constraint, however, changes in prices must be accounted for. Deflating the minimum wage by the U.S. consumer price index allows for abstraction of purely inflationary trends in the economy from measurement of the real minimum wage. Figure 2 illustrates the trend over time in the basic minimum wage deflated by the U.S. consumer price index. The general pattern has been for the real minimum wage to increase, legislated increases

12

TABLE 1

Estimated Proportion of Nonsupervisory Employees Covered by the Basic Minimum Wage and by the Rate Applicable to Newly Covered Workers, by Industry, 1947–1978

Year	Mining CB[a]	Mining CN[b]	Contract Construction CB[a]	Contract Construction CN[b]	Manufacturing CB[a]	Manufacturing CN[b]	Transportation and Public Utilities CB[a]	Transportation and Public Utilities CN[b]	Wholesale Trade CB[a]	Wholesale Trade CN[b]	Retail Trade CB[a]	Retail Trade CN[b]	Finance, Insurance, Real Estate CB[a]	Finance, Insurance, Real Estate CN[b]	Services (Excluding Domestic) CB[a]	Services (Excluding Domestic) CN[b]
1947-1960	0.99	—	0.44	—	0.95	—	0.88	—	0.69	—	0.03	—	0.74	—	0.19	—
1961-1966	0.99	—	0.44	0.36	0.95	0.01	0.88	0.07	0.69	—	0.03	0.30	0.74	—	0.19	0.03
1967-1968	0.99	—	0.80	0.19	0.96	0.01	0.95	0.02	0.69	0.03	0.33	0.156	0.74	—	0.22	0.411
1969	0.991	—	0.825	0.164	0.964	0.004	0.957	0.026	0.727	0.035	0.330	0.253	0.753	—	0.245	0.454
1970	0.991	—	0.818	0.177	0.964	0.003	0.955	0.027	0.723	0.037	0.330	0.255	0.732	0.026	0.258	0.452
1971	0.991	—	0.826	0.169	0.963	0.004	0.954	0.025	0.725	0.036	0.339	0.264	0.732	0.026	0.269	0.438
1972	0.991	—	0.820	0.175	0.964	0.004	0.954	0.024	0.725	0.035	0.348	0.268	0.733	0.026	0.269	0.436
1973	0.991	—	0.819	0.176	0.964	0.003	0.950[c]	0.030[c]	0.733[c]	0.028[c]	0.375	0.268	0.732	0.028	0.269	0.441
1974	0.993	—	0.806	0.189	0.968	0.006[d]	0.953	0.029	0.770	0.030	0.373	0.264[d]	0.733	0.029	0.277	0.441[d]
1975	0.994	—	0.812	0.182	0.968	0.006	0.957	0.026	0.770	0.030	0.361	0.303	0.733	0.029	0.275	0.443
1976	0.994	—	0.812	0.182	0.968	0.006	0.958	0.025	0.770	0.030	0.372	0.347	0.733	0.029	0.280	0.440
1977	0.995	—	0.813	0.182	0.967	0.006	0.959	0.023	0.770	0.030	0.376	0.405	0.733	0.029	0.284	0.453
1978	0.995	—	0.995	—	0.972	—	0.992	—	0.798	—	0.783	0.014	0.759	—	0.759	0.004

[a] Proportion of nonsupervisory employees covered by the basic minimum.

[b] Proportion of nonsupervisory employees covered by the rate applicable to newly covered workers for 1961–1977. In 1978, the proportion of workers who may be subject to a lower minimum wage as a result of changes in section 3(s) of the Fair Labor Standards Act.

[c] Data for coverage shifted from wholesale trade to the transportation industry.

[d] Includes employment subject to the minimum wage as of May 1974.

Source: Employment Standards Administration Division of Evaluation and Research, April 25, 1979.

13

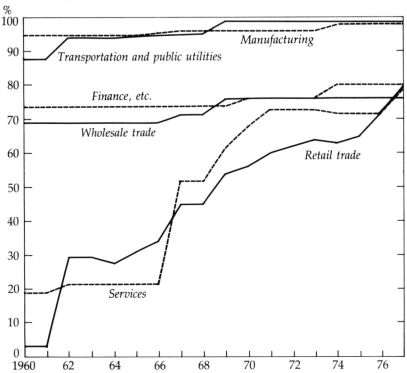

FIGURE 1

PERCENTAGE OF EMPLOYMENT COVERED BY FEDERAL
MINIMUM-WAGE LEGISLATION, BY INDUSTRY, 1960–1977

in the federal minimum wage causing it to rise, sometimes dramatically, and general increases in prices lowering it.

A measure often used to deflate the nominal minimum wage is the average manufacturing wage. Figure 3 presents the time pattern of the ratio of the national basic minimum wage to the average manufacturing wage. This measure, it is argued, captures not only effects of changes in overall price levels but also the increased productivity of labor, which also should serve to reduce the impact of the minimum wage on employment. Two shortcomings plague this measure as an indicator of the effective level of the minimum, however. First, increased productivity may very well apply only to those workers who remain employed; low-skill workers disemployed by the minimum do not have the chance for on-the-job training and hence do not increase in productivity as do those who are employed. The effective minimum wage for these workers should not reflect increases in productivity of other workers. A second and more se-

14

TABLE 2

FEDERAL MINIMUM-WAGE LEVELS AND ESTIMATED NUMBERS OF
EMPLOYEES COVERED BY THE FLSA

Effective Date of Minimum-Wage Change and Coverage Category	Minimum- Wage Rate	Estimated Number of Covered Employees (thousands)[a]
October 24, 1938	$0.25	11,000
October 24, 1939	0.30	12,548
October 24, 1945	0.40	20,000
January 25, 1950	0.75	20,933
March 1, 1955	1.00	23,976
September 3, 1961		27,478
Covered prior to 1961 amendments	1.15	23,854
Newly covered by 1961 amendments	1.00	3,624
September 3, 1963		
Covered prior to 1961 amendments	1.25	23,900
September 3, 1964		
Newly covered by 1961 amendments	1.15	3,600
September 3, 1965		29,593
Newly covered by 1961 amendments	1.25	3,600
February 1, 1967		40,434
Covered prior to 1966 amendments	1.40	32,307
Newly covered nonfarm and farm[b]	1.00	8,127
February 1, 1968		41,562
Covered prior to 1966 amendments	1.60	33,052
Newly covered nonfarm and farm[b]	1.15	8,510
February 1, 1969		44,569
Newly covered nonfarm and farm	1.30	10,356
February 1, 1970		46,255
Newly covered nonfarm only	1.45	10,889
February 1, 1971		45,511
Newly covered nonfarm only	1.60	11,261
May 1, 1974		56,112
Nonfarm		
Covered prior to 1966 amendments	2.00	37,124
Covered as a result of the 1966 amendments	1.90	11,790
Covered as a result of the 1974 amendments[c]	1.90	6,660
Farm	1.60	538
January 1, 1975		57,342
Nonfarm		
Covered prior to 1966 amendments	2.10	37,650

15

TABLE 2 (continued)

Effective Date of Minimum-Wage Change and Coverage Category	Minimum-Wage Rate	Estimated Number of Covered Employees (thousands)[a]
Covered as a result of the 1966 amendments	2.00	12,345
Covered as a result of the 1974 amendments[c]	2.00	6,760
Farm	1.80	587
January 1, 1976		56,121
Nonfarm		
Covered prior to 1966 amendments	2.30	35,677
Covered as a result of the 1966 amendments	2.30	12,806
Covered as a result of the 1974 amendments[c]	2.20	7,041
Farm	2.00	597
January 1, 1977		51,875
Nonfarm		
Covered as a result of the 1966 amendments[d]	2.30	10,472
Covered as a result of the 1974 amendments[d]	2.30	3,830
Farm	2.20	640
January 1, 1978[d]	2.65	54,446
January 1, 1979[d]	2.90	57,343

[a] The estimated number of covered employees listed in this column pertains specifically to the date and coverage category listed on the left-hand side of the table. Where no specific coverage category is listed, the coverage estimate refers to all covered employment.

[b] Excludes retail and service employees added to coverage by the 1966 amendments who became subject to the minimum-wage provisions of the Fair Labor Standards Act on February 1, 1969.

[c] Excludes retail and service workers in multiunit enterprises who became subject at a later date as a result of the phase-out of the minimum-wage exemption under section 13(a)(2).

[d] Excludes state and local government employees engaged in activities that are an integral part of traditional government functions but that the Supreme Court ruled to be outside the scope of the minimum-wage and overtime provisions of the Fair Labor Standards Act.

SOURCE: Employment Standards Administration Division of Evaluation and Research, February 9, 1979.

rious flaw in this measure is that increases in the minimum wage serve to increase the measured average manufacturing hourly wage. The lowest-skill workers are those most likely to be disemployed in the manufacturing sector because of the minimum wage. The average manufacturing wage measures wages for those remaining employed

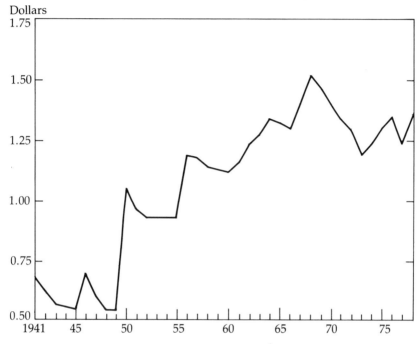

FIGURE 2
BASIC FEDERAL MINIMUM WAGE
DEFLATED BY U.S. CONSUMER PRICE INDEX, 1941–1978

NOTE: 1967 = 1.00

(above the minimum), with increases in the minimum no longer including low-wage workers in the calculation of the average wage. An increase in the minimum wage serves to increase the measured average hourly wage, especially for those industries that employ a large number of lower-skill, lower-wage workers. Further, an increase in the minimum wage may serve to increase the wage of those remaining employed, the so-called ripple effect. If low-skill workers are disemployed by the minimum wage, the value of higher-skill workers is enhanced, leading to increased wages for those remaining employed. The average manufacturing wage itself is potentially affected by the level of the minimum wage. If increases in the level of the minimum wage increase the average manufacturing wage, the ratio of the two will understate the magnitude of changes in the minimum wage itself. Comparison of figures 2 and 3 shows that although both indexes move together, the magnitude of changes

17

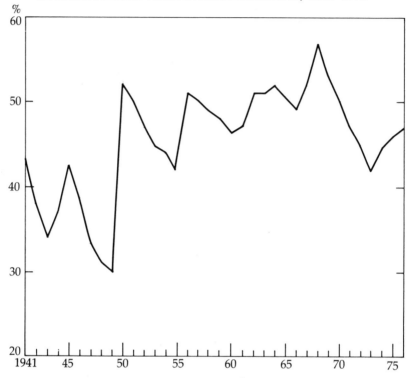

differs. This book examines the impact of changes in the minimum
wage and coverage on workers' compensation and the skill composition of employment. To the extent that average wage measures
are affected by these factors, the index shown in figure 3 misrep-
resents the nature of the minimum-wage constraint.

State Minimum-Wage Legislation

Federal minimum-wage legislation applies to those employers and
employees not subject to higher state minimum wages, although in
some cases state legislation specifically exempts employees covered
by federal law, preventing the higher state minimum from applying.
Because of incomplete coverage under federal legislation, however,
state minimums, even if less than federal, still play a potentially
important role in measuring the extent to which minimum-wage
constraints apply to economic activity.

18

Table 3 presents estimates of federal and state coverage under minimum-wage legislation as of 1970. More than one-third of those not covered by federal law were covered by state legislation, in some cases because state minimum wages were higher than the federal and in other cases because state coverage provisions applied to individuals not covered by federal law. The majority of those covered by state minimums are in retail trade and service sectors, the areas least covered under federal legislation. While state coverage is often a small percentage of combined state and federal coverage, the number of workers covered by state legislation is often a high percentage of those workers not covered by federal standards.

Combined State and Federal Legislation

A potentially important effect of minimum-wage legislation (which covers only some sectors of economic activity) is that low-skill, low-wage workers gain employment in the uncovered sectors, though possibly at lower wages than before. With increased coverage (stemming from state and federal legislation), however, this opportunity for continued employment may be very much decreased. Hence the effects of federal minimum-wage legislation will differ among states because of variation in state legislation; for some states the measures of coverage presented in figure 1 will be appropriate, while for others the extent of coverage in each sector may be high for the entire period.

Even in the absence of state minimum-wage legislation, differences among states in industry composition will lead to differences in the extent of coverage because of variation in federal coverage by industry (figure 1). Total coverage in a particular state will change more or less than total coverage based on national figures, depending on the composition of employment among industries in the state. Moreover, coverage based on size of firms' sales means that employment in areas with more small firms relative to the rest of the industry will be covered less than national figures indicate.

In addition to differences in coverage and minimum-wage levels among states, there are also differences in cost-of-living indexes among states. The time pattern of the real minimum wage presented in figure 2 is based on the national consumer price index, which captures general increases in prices over time. At any point in time, however, the national minimum is a higher effective minimum wage in an area where wages and prices would be low in the absence of any wage restrictions. This would serve to shift the curve in figure

TABLE 3

Employees Covered by Federal and State Minimum-Wage Legislation as of February 1, 1970
(in thousands)

Industry	Total Number of Nonsupervisory Employees	Total Number of Employees Covered by the FLSA	Number of Employees Covered by State Laws Only[a]	State Coverage as a Percentage of Total Coverage	State Coverage as a Percentage of Employees Not Covered by the FLSA
Total private sector	54,897	43,114	4,107	8.7	34.9
Agriculture, forestry, and fisheries	1,273	620	82	11.7	12.6
Mining	570	565	2	0.4	40.0
Contract construction	3,444	3,409	11	0.3	31.5
Manufacturing	18,381	17,793	99	0.6	16.8
Transportation, communications, utilities	4,164	4,095	35	0.8	50.7
Wholesale trade	3,524	2,686	66	2.4	7.9
Retail trade	9,948	5,803	2,258	28.0	54.5
Finance, insurance, real estate	3,119	2,349	141	5.7	18.3
Services (excluding domestic service)	8,289	5,794	1,413	19.6	56.6

NOTE: Figures are estimated on the basis of 1969 employment data.

[a] Estimates of coverage by state minimum-wage laws are only for those states that had wage laws or orders enacted or revised from 1962 to December 1, 1969.

SOURCE: "Estimates of Coverage under the Minimum Wage and Overtime Standards of the Fair Labor Standards Act and State Labor Standards Laws as of February 1, 1970," U.S. Department of Labor, Wage and Hour Division (August 1970).

2 up in these areas and down in high price areas, proportionate to the cost-of-living differences.

Summary

Under federal minimum-wage legislation, employment coverage has increased since the early 1960s in conjunction with variations in the level of the minimum wage. This increased coverage has replaced coverage under state minimum-wage legislation in many cases. Regional variation in industrial composition and costs of living, in conjunction with state legislation, suggests that federal minimum-wage legislation is likely to have impacts that differ depending on location of employment. Measurement of the effects of national minimum-wage regulations needs to take such differences into account in order to determine who benefits and who loses because of such legislation.

3
Framework

Federal minimum-wage legislation has been characterized by increased coverage of employment in more industries and by variation in the level of the real minimum wage. We need to develop a methodology for examining the varied impacts of such developments that will take into account differences in worker skills and implications of these differences, making it possible to determine who benefits and who loses as a result of minimum-wage legislation. This chapter presents a summary of the issues involved with minimum wages, abstracting from regional implications. The impacts of minimum wages arise from the regulation of labor market conditions. Direct impacts on employment and earnings of workers depend on the level of the minimum wage and the extent to which it is imposed on the economy. Further impacts on product markets depend on the nature of product demand and the manner in which inputs not constrained by the minimum wage interact with labor skills in production. Building on this framework, chapter 4 extends the analysis to examine impacts in a diverse spatial economy more fully.[1]

Labor Market Conditions

An effective minimum-wage constraint essentially limits employment in covered sectors to workers with an hourly wage (subject to the associated overtime regulations) greater than or equal to the minimum wage. With complete coverage the minimum applies to a par-

[1] The discussion in this and the following chapter is based on the model developed in appendix A. The distinction between a nonspatial national economy and one with economic activity dispersed among many areas within a nation is not so different from consideration of a world economy ignoring variation among nations. The discussion presented in this chapter is very much applicable to effects on international trade of minimum wages applied to individual nations.

ticular person regardless of his type of occupation or the type of industry in which he is employed.[2] With incomplete coverage the minimum applies to a particular person only if he is employed in the covered sector. The effectiveness of the minimum in the latter case is less binding for a given worker because it applies only to employment conditions in particular industries, with type of employer (not necessarily type of occupation) determining applicability of the minimum-wage constraint. Hence switching industry of employment allows for a potentially large reduction in the binding nature of a minimum wage on a particular worker's wage.

The demand for labor stems from the usefulness of labor services in production of goods and services. Labor services in turn depend on the types and levels of skills possessed by workers. Some industries may have little use for some particular types of worker skills while being very dependent on other types of worker skills. An individual worker may possess a variety of skills, some of which are specific to a particular firm or industry and others of which are general among industries. Industry demands for types of worker skills interact with the supply of these skills by workers, determining who is employed where and at what wage. Since some types of skills are demanded by many types of industries, labor market conditions for workers possessing these skills are not industry-specific. Rather, with flows of workers among industries, employment conditions are determined by the whole set of industries that demand labor skills and by the supply of labor skills, only a part of which may be firm- or industry-specific. This situation is depicted in figure 4, where the demand for labor skills is the sum of all industry demands. As the return to skills increases, more workers will choose to enter the labor market, and possibly those already working will work more hours. Increased returns to skill act to increase the quantity of skills supplied in the labor market, as shown by the upward-sloping supply curve of skills. Industry demand for skills is downward sloping, with increased costs of worker skills leading to a lower quantity demanded. The intersection of demand and supply determines the price of a unit of skill, P, and the total level of skill employed in the market, S.

---

[2] Complete coverage is taken here to mean that the minimum wage applies to employment of a particular worker in any industry and to all types of workers and their occupations in a particular industry. The only uncovered sectors or occupations are those involved in household production. Incomplete coverage here is regarded as the absence of a minimum wage in a particular industry regardless of worker characteristics or occupation type.

FIGURE 4
Supply and Demand of Worker Skills

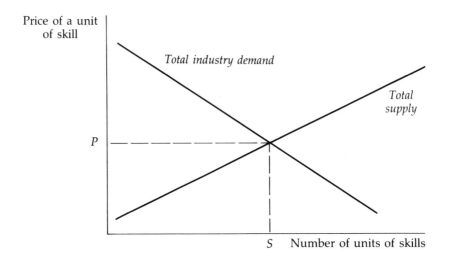

Skill Differences among Workers

Variation among workers in types of skills possessed provides one means of classifying workers into different groups that is useful for distinguishing between those directly affected by minimum-wage legislation and those only indirectly affected. In terms of figure 4, the price per unit of skill may be so high for a particular type of skill that all workers having some of this ability are highly paid. Similarly, each worker supplying such skill may be very skillful and hence be highly paid. Some jobs require skills so costly to obtain that wages of workers in these occupations are very high. Many of these skills might be obtained through formal education, or perhaps some individuals are endowed with them at birth. Those entering the labor market start with relatively high levels of skill and associated high wages. On the other hand, some jobs require skills of other sorts that are not costly to obtain and are supplied at lower prices. Lower wages, in general associated with workers in these occupations, suggest that minimum-wage standards more directly affect the latter workers than those in occupations with generally higher wages.

Occupational distinctions facilitate general statements about who loses and who benefits from minimum wages by types of occupation. Once differences in skill levels have been determined for workers within occupations, more refined implications may be apparent. For

FIGURE 5
DISTRIBUTION OF WORKERS BY SKILL LEVEL

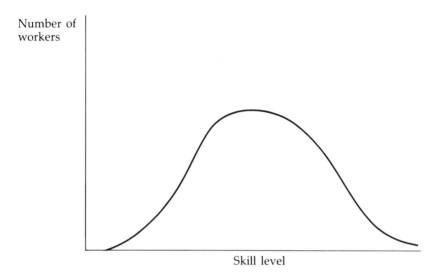

Number of workers

Skill level

any occupation formal schooling may increase the starting skill levels. Moreover, on-the-job training may enhance skills. Hence within job categories people may possess different levels of the relevant skill at any point in time, with wage differences reflecting relative skill levels among workers.

The supply of worker skill shown in figure 4 depends on the number of workers and the skill per worker. While the price per unit of skill is determined by the total supply of skill, the wage of a particular worker depends on the market-determined price per unit of skill and the individual's skill level. Figure 5 presents a hypothetical distribution of number of workers according to skill in a particular occupation that makes up S in figure 4. Each individual at the lower end of the skill distribution provides only a small part of total skills in the economy, while those at the upper end provide a large part of total skills. The number of workers employed is equal to the sum of workers at each skill level, the area under the curve in figure 5. Total skills employed (equal to S in figure 4), however, are equal to the sum of all workers at a particular skill level times the skill possessed. Hence the number of skills employed could remain the same if many low-skill workers were replaced with a few higher-skill workers.

Given the price per unit of skill determined by market demand and supply of worker skills, and given the distribution of skills

FIGURE 6
DISTRIBUTION OF WORKERS BY WAGE

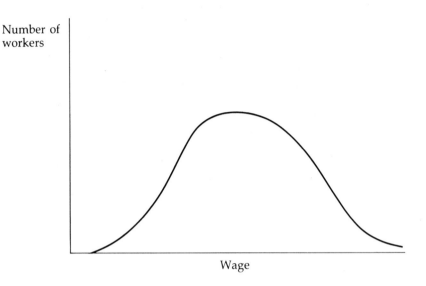

Number of workers

Wage

among workers that makes up total skills employed, the distribution of wages among workers is determined. The form of the wage distribution is the same as that of the skill distribution, with workers who have twice the level of skills as others having twice the wage as well. The wage distribution resulting from figures 4 and 5 is illustrated in figure 6. If the skill distribution in figure 5 remains the same, an increase in the price per unit of skill, P, shifts the wage distribution proportionately to the right, increasing wages of higher-skill workers by more than those of low-skill workers.

Demand and supply of various types of skills determine the wage distribution for each type of skill in a way analogous to that shown in figure 6. Wage differences between workers of different occupations depend on total demand and supply of skills in the occupations as well as on the levels of skills possessed by the workers.

A single industry in the economy makes up only a part of the demand for skills in figure 4, and if workers of varying skills are mobile among industries, the price per unit of skill will be the same for that industry as for others. Moreover, the number of skills employed in that industry will be affected by the price per unit of skill only as this price affects the market as a whole.

The minimum wage is a restriction on the wage paid to an

employee in a covered industry. As such it imposes a constraint on employment of workers in the lower end of the wage distribution in figure 6 in that industry. Uncovered sectors are not restricted from employing these workers, however. If all industries are covered, the minimum-wage restriction applies to all workers below the minimum, regardless of where they are employed.

The effects of a minimum wage on employment and compensation of workers depend on the level of the minimum wage relative to the wage distribution in figure 6, which is itself determined by total market supply and demand of skills, as depicted in figure 4, and the composition of skill levels making up the supply, in figure 5. Moreover, if not all industries are covered by the minimum wage, workers at the lower end of the wage distribution are restricted from employment at their low wage only in the covered sector, not in the market as a whole. Flows of workers of different skills among covered and uncovered industries in the presence of a minimum wage suggest an important way in which the minimum wage is ineffective in altering the employment and compensation patterns of workers.

Partial Coverage: The Early Years

Prior to the 1961 amendments, coverage under the FLSA was only partial, mostly applying to employment in manufacturing and mining industries. Under such circumstances flows of workers among industries play a major role in determining impacts of the minimum wage. In the absence of a minimum wage, both covered and uncovered industries potentially employ both high- and low-skill workers. Moreover, workers of the same skill level but employed in different industries receive the same wage. If this were not the case, industries would have an incentive to hire workers earning less than others with the same skill levels, and workers earning less than those in another industry would have an incentive to switch industry of employment. Figure 7 depicts wage distributions of workers of a particular occupation—skill type—in uncovered and covered industries before the imposition of a minimum wage.[3]

Imposition of a minimum wage, $\overline{W}$, in the covered sector means that workers previously earning less than $\overline{W}$ in a covered sector are no longer employable there at a wage less than $\overline{W}$. These workers can still be employed in the uncovered sector, however. Loss of these workers in the covered sector means that covered-sector em-

[3] For simplicity in diagramming, it is assumed that before the minimum wage is imposed, each sector (covered or uncovered) employs the same number of worker skills with the same composition.

27

FIGURE 7
Effect of a Minimum Wage on Wages and Employment in Covered and Uncovered Industries: The Case of No Worker Wage Effects

A. Uncovered industries

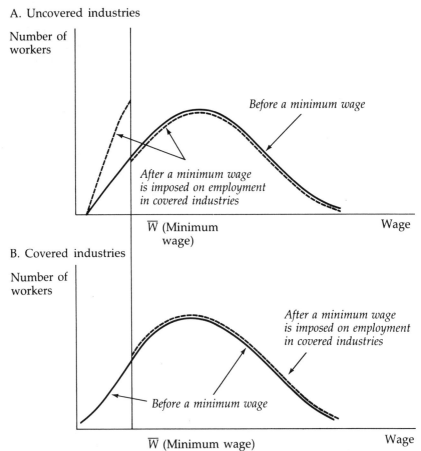

B. Covered industries

ployers have incentives to replace the lost skills with workers whose wages are greater than $\overline{W}$. Flows of low-skill workers with wages less than $\overline{W}$ out of the covered sector and into the uncovered sector are replaced with flows of some higher-skill workers out of the uncovered sector into the covered sector. The result is depicted in figure 7 by the dashed curves. The uncovered sector now employs all low-skill workers with wages less than the minimum wage and employs fewer high-skill workers with wages greater than the minimum. Similarly, the covered sector no longer employs any workers with wages less than the minimum and employs more workers with wages greater than the minimum. These shifts can take place without a change in wages for any of the workers, high or low in skill, because nothing has changed the ability of employers in either sector to hire enough skills to satisfy the quantity demanded at the prevailing price of skills.[4] Each industry can satisfy the quantity of skills demanded at the price of skills before the minimum wage, with the total market demand and supply still intersecting at P and S in figure 4. The minimum wage merely serves to alter the mix of workers in each industry without changing worker wages and without inducing unemployment.

If such a transfer is affected costlessly, no one benefits and no one gains from the minimum-wage constraint. While there are no ill effects, there are no benefits.[5] On the other hand, fixed costs of changing jobs would impose net costs on the economy without benefits for any of the workers concerned.[6] Because of differences in worker skills, some of which result in wages above the minimum wage, that are demanded by industries in both covered and uncovered sectors, replacement of low-wage, low-skill workers with high-wage, high-skill workers in the covered sector results in little real impact on employment and earnings of workers in either sector.

Complete Coverage: The Trend

Since the early 1960s, as examined in chapter 2, federal minimum-wage legislation has increased coverage to more industries. On the one hand, this is captured in figure 7 by reducing the size of the uncovered sector, but once the uncovered sector becomes very small, there are not enough high-skill workers in the entire economy merely to replace the skills of those previously earning less than $\overline{W}$ in the covered sector. To illustrate the nature of minimum-wage impacts on employment and earnings of workers when coverage is complete, consider figure 8, which builds upon the pre-minimum-wage distribution of worker's wages of figure 6. Before imposition of the minimum wage, the wage distribution is determined from the skill dis-

[4] This would not be the case if the covered sector were extremely large relative to the uncovered sector or if the minimum were so high that there were not enough high-skill workers in both sectors previously earning more than $\overline{W}$ to replace those earning less than $\overline{W}$ in the covered sector.
[5] Industry-specific skills would serve to alter the results above somewhat. Still, the nature of redistribution of workers among covered and uncovered industries is not changed substantially.
[6] Most likely these transition costs would be partly incurred by employers and partly by employees. Disemployment of workers very low in skill would occur if the fixed transaction costs were greater than the net benefits associated with continued employment.

FIGURE 8

Effect of a Minimum Wage on Wages and Employment in a Fully Covered Economy: The Case of a Fixed Labor Force

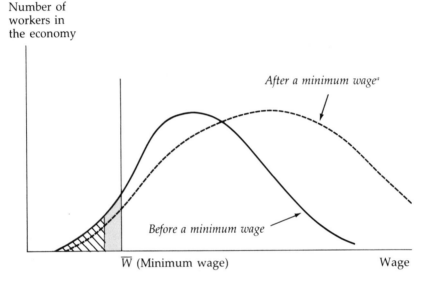

NOTE: The shaded area represents those workers who previously earned less than the minimum wage but, because of the increase in the price per unit of skill in the presence of the minimum wage, remain employed with wages above the minimum. The hatched area represents those workers who are disemployed because of the minimum wage.

[a] This is the wage distribution before the minimum wage shifted proportionately to the right because of the increase in the price per unit of skill for those workers remaining employed (the ripple effect).

tribution, from figure 5, and the price per unit of skill, from figure 4. A minimum wage of $\overline{W}$ means that all workers previously earning less than $\overline{W}$ have to be either employed at $\overline{W}$ (or an amount greater than $\overline{W}$) or not employed at all.

Three types of effects result from the imposition of a minimum wage such as $\overline{W}$ in figure 8 on a completely covered economy, and all stem from an increase in the price per unit of skill. Their different magnitudes very much affect who benefits and who loses because of the minimum wage.

The Ripple Effect. Since workers earning less than $\overline{W}$ in figure 8 cannot be employed unless their wage increases, in the absence of

30

FIGURE 9

Supply and Demand Determination of Employment and Price of a Unit of Skill in the Presence of a Minimum Wage: The Case of a Fixed Labor Force

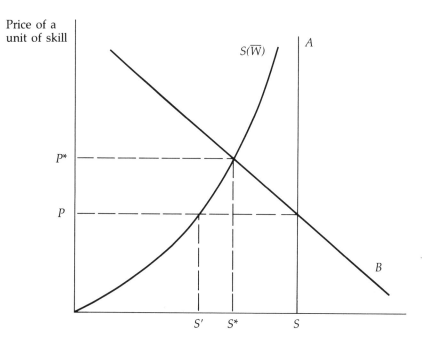

NOTE: Curve A is the supply of worker skills in the economy in the absence of a minimum wage. Curve B is the demand for worker skills in the economy. Curve $S(\overline{W})$ is the supply of worker skills in the presence of a minimum wage of $\overline{W}$, made up of those workers whose productive value is greater than the minimum wage. P is the price per unit of skill in the absence of a minimum wage. S is the number of worker skills employed in the absence of a minimum wage. P^* is the price per unit of skill after the minimum wage is imposed. S^* is the number of worker skills employed in the economy after the minimum wage is imposed. S^* is greater than S' because of the ripple effect. S' is the number of worker skills that would be employed in the economy in the presence of a minimum wage if there is no change in the price per unit of skill. This would occur if the demand for labor were flat.

a change in their productivity the supply of worker skills to the economy is less, given the minimum-wage constraint for any particular price per unit of skill. For a fixed labor force equal to that before the minimum wage, figure 9 presents the equilibrium price per unit of skill and amount of skills employed. This is the same as in figure 4 except that the supply of worker skills is fixed. Since the minimum wage disallows for employment of workers at wages less than $\overline{W}$, however, the supply of skills to the economy shifts to the left, as

31

illustrated by $S(\overline{W})$. As the price per unit of skill increases, the wage distribution in figure 8 shifts to the right, with fewer workers below the minimum wage. The curve $S(\overline{W})$ in figure 9 slopes up because increased price per unit of skill reduces the number of workers with wages less than the minimum. If the price per unit of skill were very high, even the lowest-skill workers would be worth more than the minimum wage. At low skill prices, however, more and more workers would be worth less than the minimum. Any shift to the left in supply increases the price per unit of skill because of a downward-sloping demand curve. The new price per unit of skill is given by P^* in figure 9, which is greater than the price of skill before the minimum wage and also is associated with fewer skills employed in the economy. The increase in P due to the minimum wage tends to increase the wage each worker would earn and shifts the wage distribution for existing workers to the right, as illustrated by the dashed curve in figure 8. Any level of skill still employed now receives more because of the movement up the demand curve. Under such conditions some of the workers previously earning less than the minimum wage, $\overline{W}$, are now worth more than the minimum (or equal to it), given by the shaded portion in figure 8. The skill distribution of workers has not changed, but because of disemployment of the very lowest skill workers, the returns to skills of workers remaining employed increases.

The increase in price per unit of skill (1) allows some workers previously earning less than the minimum wage to retain employment and at wages higher than before and (2) increases the wages of all higher-skill workers, who also reap the benefits of the minimum wage. Benefits to these workers arise at the expense of lost employment for those with the least skill.

Under the fixed-labor-force conditions, the flatter the demand curve in figure 9, the smaller the increase in P. While this leads to smaller benefits for higher-skill workers (their wages not increasing by as much), it also leads to a greater number of disemployed lower-skill workers. Easy substitution of other inputs (such as machinery) for these types of worker skills would tend to make this the case.[7]

Elasticity of Labor Skill Supply. The discussion above pertained to a fixed employment force where the minimum wage served to benefit those remaining employed at the expense of those unemployed. While some "lower-skill" workers previously earning just below the

[7] In addition, reductions in output in industries where these skills are employed lead to downward slopes of the demand curve in figure 4, although effects on output markets are discussed further below.

minimum wage gained, the very lowest skill workers were unambiguously harmed, losing employment opportunities. Still, the increase in returns to skill if employed in the market (the rise from P to P^* in figure 9) might lead to an increased quantity of worker skills supplied in the economy. Instead of a vertical supply of skill, as shown in figure 9, increased price per unit of skill could induce others to enter the labor market, as in figure 4. Increased labor-force participation of females in recent decades suggests that these effects may not be negligible.

Figure 10 reproduces figure 9 for workers employed before the minimum wage but allows for other workers to enter the labor force as returns to their skills increase. The net supply of worker skills is now given by the flatter upward-sloping curve $S(\overline{W}, P)$, which slopes upward because of the reduced effectiveness of the minimum wage as the price per unit of skill increases for previously employed workers and because new workers enter the labor market.

The minimum wage leads to less of an increase in P because workers previously out of the labor force are induced into employment by higher returns to their market skills, satisfying some of the demand. This means that for those workers previously in the labor market (1) there will be less increase in wages for higher-skill workers, (2) fewer workers previously making just less than the minimum wage will retain employment, and those who do will not benefit as greatly (wages will not increase as much), and (3) more low-skill workers will be unemployed. Some of the benefits of the minimum wage are obtained by those workers who enter the labor market because of enhanced wages. In terms of figure 10, $S(\overline{W}, P)$, the supply of worker skills that depends on the minimum wage, $\overline{W}$, as well as the price per unit of skills, P, intersects the demand for labor skills at a price $\overline{P}$ which is less than that when the labor force is fixed, P^*, and at a higher quantity of skills, $\overline{S}$, which is greater than S^*. The ripple effect on employment of low-skill workers previously earning less than the minimum wage is less, however. The increase in employment of skilled workers previously earning less than the minimum wage is less because the increase in the price per unit of skill is less. The increase in employment of skill services from low-skill workers previously in the labor market due to the ripple effect is now only $S' - S_0$, which is less than $S^* - S_0$, the amount if the labor force is fixed.

Most very high skill workers would already be in the labor force in the absence of the minimum wage. Those induced into the labor market are likely to have medium-level skills, with opportunities outside the labor market paying more than such workers would have

FIGURE 10

SUPPLY AND DEMAND DETERMINATION OF EMPLOYMENT AND PRICE OF A UNIT OF SKILL IN THE PRESENCE OF A MINIMUM WAGE: THE CASE OF A NONFIXED LABOR FORCE

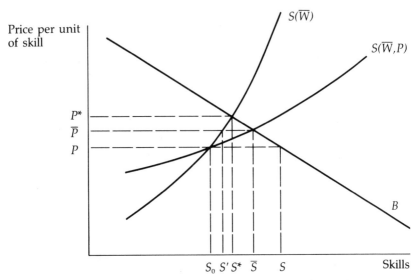

NOTE: Curve $S(\overline{W})$ is the same as in figure 9. It is the supply of worker skills in the presence of a minimum wage that stems from those workers previously in the labor market that have productive value greater than the minimum wage. $S(\overline{W},P)$ is the total supply of worker skills in the economy in the presence of a minimum wage which includes those previously in the labor market as well as new entrants with productive value greater than the minimum wage. B is the demand for worker skills. S is the number of skills employed in the absence of a minimum wage and is the same as in figure 9. P is the price per unit of skill in the absence of a minimum wage and is the same as in figure 9. S^* is the number of worker skills employed in the presence of a minimum wage when the labor force is fixed and is the same as in figure 9. P^* is the price per unit of skill in the presence of a minimum wage with a fixed labor force and is the same as in figure 9. S_0 is the number of worker skills that would be employed in the presence of a minimum wage if demand for labor were perfectly elastic. $\overline{S}$ is the number of worker skills employed in the presence of the minimum wage with a nonfixed labor force. $\overline{P}$ is the price per unit of skill in the presence of a minimum wage with a nonfixed labor force. S' is the number of worker skills that were previously in the labor market that remain employed after the minimum wage is imposed.

earned in the absence of the ripple effect on returns to market skills. Figure 11 reproduces figure 8, showing the shift to the right in the wage distribution in the case of a fixed labor force, and compares this with the situation where medium-skill workers enter the labor force because of increased market wages. The ripple effect is less with a smaller increase in wages for workers previously employed

34

FIGURE 11
EFFECT OF A MINIMUM WAGE ON WAGES
WHEN THE RIPPLE EFFECT INDUCES
ENTRY OF NEW WORKERS INTO THE LABOR MARKET

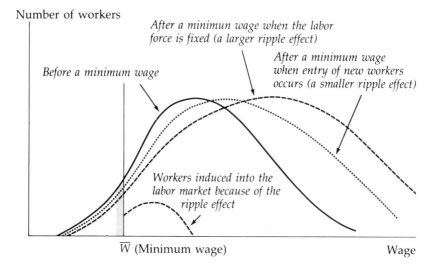

NOTE: The shaded area represents those workers who previously earned less than the minimum wage but, because of the increase in the price per unit of skill in the presence of the minimum wage, remain employed with wages above the minimum.

who remain employed, as depicted by the light curve. Fewer workers previously earning less than the minimum wage retain employment—the shaded area in figure 11 is skinnier than that in figure 8—the difference given by the additional employment of medium-skill workers who enter the labor market, depicted by the light dashed curve in figure 11.

Output Market Impacts

The minimum wage, as a direct regulation of labor employment conditions, affects output markets and other input markets only through their connectedness with labor inputs. Substitution and complementarity among different types of skills directly affected by the minimum-wage constraint could exacerbate or mitigate the impact on any single skill type, but the workers who lose are those with the lowest skill levels. While minimum-wage legislation is usually applied to all workers within a covered industry, some types of skills may not be directly affected at all, with substitution for or complementarity with affected skill groups benefiting or hurting returns to workers of these types. Nonlabor inputs such as machinery (also produced in the covered manufacturing sector) may be affected in much the same way as these high-wage occupations, with analogous increases or decreases in demand for these inputs.

Output effects of minimum wages stem from increased cost of production due to increased costs of labor skill services. In the first case considered above, where partial coverage serves only to change skill composition among sectors without affecting costs, output reductions (or interactions with other inputs) will not occur. Since the minimum wage has no real impact on labor costs, it has no further impacts on production. As coverage becomes more complete, however, output effects result from increased labor skill costs. Increases in costs of production lead to higher prices of output, which reduce consumption, depending on the sensitivity of output demand to price. If product demand were perfectly inelastic, output would not be reduced, although because of substitution of other types of inputs, the demand for labor skills such as in figure 4 might still be relatively flat. In such a case disemployment of the lowest-skill workers is large, without accrual of benefits to higher-skill workers in the same occupation. Instead, other input owners benefit, while consumers of the output lose. If there is little substitution among skills directly affected by the minimum-wage constraint and a price-insensitive demand for output, the demand for such labor skills will be less sensitive to skill costs, resulting in less disemployment of the lower-skill workers, with increased returns (higher wages) to those remaining employed. Then the losers are the consumers of the output. The more price-sensitive is product demand, the greater the reduction in output and the disemployment of lower-skill workers, and the less the ripple effect.

The conditions discussed above suggest who benefits and who pays for regulation of labor employment conditions by the minimum wage. In all cases the lowest-skill workers lose, becoming disemployed, while the size of the group depends on the elasticity of demand for skill services (which depends on substitution of other inputs and conditions in the output market) and the sensitivity with respect to market wages of entry into the labor force of higher-skill workers.

Nonwage Forms of Payment and On-the-Job Training

The minimum wage itself serves only as a limitation on monetary wages paid to workers. In the absence of any other types of regulatory restrictions on employment conditions, nonwage components of total worker's compensation would be altered so as to reduce harmful impacts of minimum-wage legislation. From the employer's point of view, the incentive for this type of avoidance practice depends on the increase in costs per unit of skill relative to costs associated with altering the wage and nonwage composition of total worker's compensation. Low-skill workers who would otherwise be disemployed because of the minimum wage have incentives to reduce nonwage forms of compensation and increase wages so as to remain employable. The costs incurred in effecting the compensation bundle composition relative to the benefits of not being employed (such as welfare payments and so forth), however, will most likely be highest for the very lowest skill group, resulting in its disemployment.

Adjustments of wage and nonwage forms of worker's compensation may reduce the disemployment impacts of a minimum wage and reduce wage increases for those who would otherwise remain employed. Although the net resource costs induced by the minimum wage can be reduced by these types of avoidance practices, real costs are incurred in such adjustment procedures, and all those remaining employed are not necessarily better off than before.

A particularly relevant nonwage characteristic of employment is associated with on-the-job training, where a worker is jointly employed and trained in a particular occupation. In essence the worker pays, through reduced compensation, for training. This means that the wage paid is less than that which the worker could earn if the training component of employment were reduced. Consider the case depicted in figure 12, which compares the wage distribution of workers when on-the-job training is taking place (some lower-skill workers accept lower current wages to pay for enhanced skills and hence increased future earnings) and when no on-the-job training occurs. For this simple case the wage distribution shifts to the right when on-the-job training no longer occurs. A minimum wage of $\overline{W}$ in a fully covered economy, ignoring the ripple effect for graphic illustration, allows some workers who previously earned less than $\overline{W}$ because of on-the-job training to retain employment but at the loss of training. Those workers in the shaded region in figure 12 would be disemployed if their wages accurately reflected their skill levels. Still, they can reduce training so as to be paid a wage equal to the minimum and remain employed. This leads to a mass of workers paid exactly the minimum wage, which is represented by a spike in the wage distribution in figure 12. Those at the lowest end of the shaded area have to give up a greater portion of their training to

FIGURE 12
EFFECT OF A MINIMUM WAGE ON WAGES AND EMPLOYMENT
IN THE PRESENCE OF ON-THE-JOB TRAINING

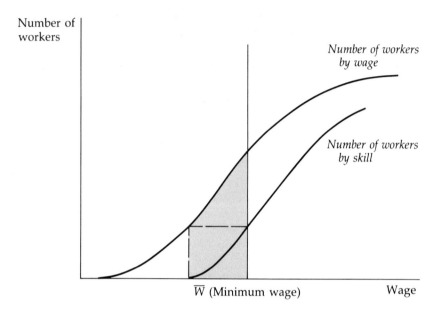

NOTE: The shaded area represents those workers who would have earned less than the minimum wage but still remain employed by sacrificing on-the-job training for current wages in the presence of a minimum wage.

remain employed, while those previously earning just less than the minimum, even with on-the-job training, have to give up less. All workers in the shaded area lose, however, even though they may remain employed. These workers sacrifice future earnings that are greater in value than increased wage income in the present.[8]

An impact of the minimum wage not captured by mere employment loss in the current period is the reduction of skill in the future for those giving up training in order to remain employed.

Summary

The discussion above has focused on the question of who is likely to benefit and lose from minimum-wage legislation. Flows of workers

[8] The increased wage income could be used to obtain skills through other sources not tied to employment—formal education and so forth. The fact that this was not done before the minimum wage constraint was imposed, however, means that it is not as appropriate as a situation of tied training and employment opportunities.

of various skills among covered and uncovered sectors allow for reduced impacts of a minimum wage on employment and earnings of workers in the presence of only partial coverage. While artificially segmenting employment of workers of different skills, if mobility of workers among industries is not extremely costly, a minimum wage applied to only one sector of the economy results in little in the way of benefits or costs to workers. When coverage is very high or complete, a minimum wage serves to disemploy the lowest-skill workers, with higher-skill workers benefiting in terms of higher wages due to the ripple effect. Moreover, entry into the labor market of new workers induced through these higher market wages increases the magnitude of disemployment of low-skill workers and reduces the benefits accruing to previously employed higher-skill workers.

4

Minimum-Wage Impacts in a Diverse Spatial Economy

The premise of the FLSA is that interstate trade and competition are adversely affected by labor market conditions that the federal minimum wage is intended to alleviate. Whether or not the minimum wage does "improve" the working of labor markets is one issue. The discussion in chapter 3 suggests that in the presence of incomplete coverage, flows of both high- and low-skill workers among industries lessen the effects on worker employment and compensation patterns. These flows result because the supply of labor skills is not totally industry-specific. Rather, labor market conditions are set by the supply of labor skills in the economy and the sum of all industry demands. Coverage of industries by minimum-wage legislation because their products are traded among states when there are other uncovered industries is likely not to affect the wages of low-skill workers.

Another issue is whether or not the minimum wage itself alters location decisions of population and employers, thereby reducing efficient allocation of resources among areas and hampering useful regional dispersion of economic activity. Just as the supply of labor skills is not industry-specific, neither is it location-specific. As in the case where workers are mobile among industry sectors within an economy, this flexibility changing the manner in which minimum wages affect employment and earnings, workers as well as industries may be mobile among regions, further altering the nature of minimum-wage impacts.

The national minimum wage is applied uniformly among areas that differ in composition of industry as well as wage levels. The extent of coverage under federal minimum-wage legislation in an area depends on industry composition because federal coverage differs among industry types. Variation among areas in costs of purchasing local goods and services as well as location-specific amenities such as pleasant climate can lead to differences in wage levels among areas. An individual worker may be indifferent to a choice between a five-dollar hourly wage in Chicago and a three-dollar hourly wage in Sun City because costs of living are less in Sun City and the amenities (sunshine) that may be consumed in Sun City are greater than those in Chicago. The two-dollar difference in hourly wage between Chicago and Sun City is that amount needed to compensate the worker, so that he will be indifferent to a choice between living and working in one area and the other. The national minimum wage is applied uniformly in Chicago and Sun City, however. As a result, the real minimum wage is higher in areas like Sun City and lower in areas like Chicago.

This chapter extends the framework discussed in chapter 3 to any economy with spatial differences in industry composition and wage differences due to variation in costs of living and amenity levels among areas.

An Overview of Location of People and Jobs

The reasons for dispersion of economic activity and population among areas within the U.S. are multifaceted. Prominent in determining location of manufacturing industry are production advantages in particular areas in conjunction with costs of transporting inputs and outputs among regions. Manufacturing industries often sell their outputs in a national market, even though production is concentrated in particular areas. Choice of location depends on costs of production as well as on the price received for output in one region compared with others. Inherent as a consideration in choice of location for manufacturing production is location of demand for labor skills in the manufacturing sector. Employment of workers in a region is tied to the location of these workers' demand for consumption goods and services.

Location of industries that do not rely as heavily on area-specific production advantages—more footloose and fancy free—is much more sensitive to demand-oriented factors. Location decisions of much of the service, retail trade, wholesale trade, and finance sectors of the economy are based on characteristics of local market demand.

In many cases factors affecting location of manufacturing industries greatly affect location of other industries and the resulting demand for labor skills. The decision to locate a large manufacturing plant in an area brings with it demand for labor skills. The workers employed in the manufacturing plant demand local goods and services and thereby induce demand for more workers employed in production of these goods and services, who in turn demand local goods and services, and so on. Hence the location of manufacturing

41

employment, more tied to location cost advantages, very much affects the location of total employment and population in the United States.

Changes in comparative cost advantages among areas change incentives for the location of production. Table 4 illustrates regional shares of employment in a variety of industries and shows how these changed over the period 1963 to 1977. Regional shares change, sometimes dramatically, over time, suggesting that industry location changes are important. One component of production cost is that associated with labor skills, which varies among regions because of cost-of-living and amenity differences. The minimum wage, while potentially affecting employment and earnings of workers in a region, may also serve to change the relative costs of labor skills among regions, thereby changing the patterns of industry location. Labor costs are a major share of total costs for many industries, small changes in labor costs in one area relative to another leading to large shifts in industry location. The national minimum wage, applied uniformly among regions that would otherwise differ in nominal costs of labor, potentially imposes differential changes in labor costs and hence incentives for movement of industry.

Industrial location changes may be slow to respond to changing regional incentives because of large fixed costs of moving. Migration of people is much less hampered by such fixed costs, however, possibly responding more rapidly to changing conditions among areas. Table 5 presents net migration patterns of the population by region for 1960–1970. These numbers indicate that substantial shifts in the location of population have been occurring. The figures show that population has dramatically increased in the West and less so in the South, relative to their previous shares. Still, these numbers capture only the net result of all population location changes. Gross flows of population both in and out of these regions are partially offsetting; so the figures in table 5 do not capture the total mobility of population. Even so, the substantial scale of net migration indicates a quite mobile population and labor force. The minimum wage, as it alters employment and earning opportunities among regions, is likely to induce migration in the setting of a mobile population and labor force.

The Impacts of Minimum Wages

State Minimum Wage Legislation in Conjunction with Federal Legislation. State minimum-wage laws are binding when they exceed federal standards. While in some cases state minimum-wage levels

TABLE 4

Manufacturing Employment, by Region, 1963 and 1977

	North-east	Middle Atlantic	East North-Central	West North-Central	South Atlantic	East South-Central	West South-Central	Mountain	Pacific	Total
Employment (in thousands)										
1963	1,425	4,075	4,483	1,014	2,125	892	865	284	1,799	16,962
1977	1,407	3,749	4,999	1,304	2,755	1,325	1,446	467	2,276	19,727
Share of U.S. total (percent)										
1963	8.4	24.0	26.4	6.0	12.5	5.3	5.1	1.7	10.6	100
1977	7.1	19.0	25.3	6.6	14.0	6.7	7.3	2.4	11.5	100
Percent change in share of U.S. total, 1963–77	−15.5	−20.8	−4.2	10.0	12.0	26.4	43.1	41.2	8.5	—

SOURCE: U.S. Census of Manufacturers (1963, 1977).

43

TABLE 5

NET MIGRATION OF THE POPULATION, BY REGION, 1960–1970

Region	Net Migration	Net Migration as a Percentage of Population
Northeast	344,330	0.7
New England	307,329	2.7
Middle Atlantic	37,001	0.1
North-central	− 763,710	− 1.3
East north-central	− 159,936	− 0.4
West north-central	− 603,774	− 3.6
South	740,364	1.2
South Atlantic	1,396,929	4.8
East south-central	− 697,512	− 5.2
West south-central	40,947	0.2
West	2,892,903	9.1
Mountain	326,441	4.1
Pacific	2,566,462	10.7

SOURCE: G. Bowles, C. Beal, and E. Lee, *Net Migration of the Population 1960–1970 by Age, Sex and Color* (Washington, D.C.: Economic Research Service, U.S. Department of Agriculture, 1975), pp. 3–9.

have exceeded those set by amendments to the FLSA, more important is that statutory state minimum wages apply to those workers not covered by federal legislation. Increased coverage under federal minimum-wage provisions has been in part only replacement of individual state provisions, though usually at higher wage levels. Changes in federal standards in the presence of already existing state legislation have much less real impact than in the case when those workers not previously covered by federal minimum wages were not covered by other state provisions.

As illustrated in chapter 3, the extent to which employment is covered in an area (for example, a particular state) is an important determinant of whether or not a minimum wage is effective in altering employment and earnings of workers. National coverage estimates presented in chapter 2 are lower bounds with respect to coverage when state legislation is present. Hence, besides differences in employment coverage under the FLSA among regions due to differences in industry composition, state minimum-wage legislation further increases coverage of employment under minimum-wage restrictions.

Complete coverage in one region in the absence of flows of workers among areas means that increases in the minimum wage in that state lead to increased costs of labor skills and disemployment of lower-skill workers. With mobility of workers among regions (migration) similar to that among industries, however, those low-skill workers disemployed in the fully covered state could obtain jobs in uncovered industries in other states. The increased returns to skill for higher-skill workers in the fully covered state offer an incentive for high-skill workers in other states to migrate into the fully covered state. In essence, differences in coverage among states due to the differential coverage of employment by federal and state minimum-wage legislation could lead to a reduced impact on employment and earnings of low- and high-skill workers because of migration between states, just as in the case of flows of workers among covered and uncovered industries. Only when coverage is high in all industries in all states will changes in minimum wages in a single region lead to further impacts on employment and earnings of workers.

Differences in Nominal Wages among Areas. Sometimes large and often persistent differentials in nominal wages characterize the regional dispersion of employment. While some of the disparities reflect differences in types of skills employed among areas, for a particular industry wage differences among areas are more likely to reflect compensation for the regionally varying cost of living.[1] Given such regional differences, a uniform national minimum wage is a higher real-wage restriction in otherwise low-nominal-wage areas and lower in otherwise high-nominal-wage areas. This implies that workers of higher skill levels are directly affected by the national minimum in areas where wages would otherwise be low, as compared with higher-wage areas.

Consider one type of industry that produces in two areas with different nominal costs of labor.[2] For simplicity in diagramming, let the same number of workers with the same skill levels be employed

[1] The appropriate cost-of-living index would include the valuation of consumption of nonmarket goods (such as sunshine). The use of the term "cost of living" in the rest of this monograph includes the valuation of amenities, as such cost-of-living differences among areas determine equilibrium nominal wage differences among areas for a particular worker.
[2] This means that the area with high labor cost has other advantages that offset their disadvantage—lower cost of other inputs, a higher received price or output, or more desirable natural conditions such as moderate climate.

FIGURE 13
Effect of a National Minimum Wage on Wages and Employment in High- and Low-Cost-of-Living Regions: The Ripple Effect without Flows of Workers between Regions

A. High-cost-of-living regions

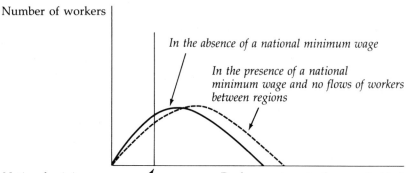

Number of workers

In the absence of a national minimum wage

In the presence of a national minimum wage and no flows of workers between regions

National minimum wage divided by the high-cost-of-living deflator

Real wage (nominal wage divided by high-cost-of-living deflator)

B. Low-cost-of-living regions

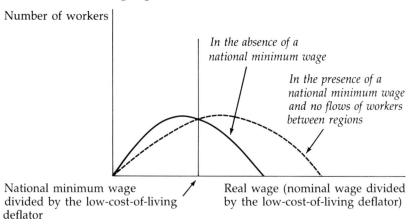

Number of workers

In the absence of a national minimum wage

In the presence of a national minimum wage and no flows of workers between regions

National minimum wage divided by the low-cost-of-living deflator

Real wage (nominal wage divided by the low-cost-of-living deflator)

in each region. This situation is depicted in figure 13, where the high-nominal-wage region is given in part (A) and the low-nominal-wage region is shown in part (B). Even though nominal wages differ among regions, they are the same in real terms—after dividing by the region-specific cost-of-living index. A uniform national minimum

46

wage of $\overline{W}$ is a higher real-minimum-wage constraint in the low-wage area, as illustrated in figure 13.

Initial Impacts. When coverage under the minimum wage is only partial, flows of higher- and lower-skill workers within a region can take place, resulting in no substantial losses or benefits due to the minimum. Each region's labor force can adjust independently of other regions, as did the labor force considered in chapter 3.[3] Still, when all workers in all areas are covered by the federal minimum wage, potentially severe regional differences in effects are possible. If demand for labor services is the same in both regions and the labor force is fixed, the ripple effect will be larger in the low-wage region. This is illustrated in figure 14, where initially demand (in terms of deflated wages) and supply of worker skills are the same before the minimum wage is instituted. The minimum wage, by directly including more workers below it in the low-wage region, creates a larger ripple effect than in the high-wage region, as the price per unit of skill is increased by more in the low-wage region. The resulting shifts in the wage distribution are shown by the dashed curves in figure 13.

If workers and industry could not migrate among areas, higher-skill workers would gain much more in lower-nominal-wage areas than in high-wage areas. On the other hand, more very low skill workers are disemployed in the low-wage area. Moreover, with the demand curve including output effects, less will be produced, and at higher prices, in the low-wage area. An extreme case is where no workers are directly affected in some high-nominal-wage areas, all the costs and benefits occurring only in low-wage areas where the minimum is effective.

Flows of Workers. As illustrated in figure 13, some workers who are not employed in the low-wage region could be employed in the high-wage region. Simply by moving to the high-wage region, they increase their nominal wage, possibly enough to be employable at or above the minimum-wage level. In addition, high-skill workers in the high-wage region could increase their real wage by moving to the low-wage region, where returns to worker skills increase by more as a result of the minimum wage.

---

[3] It is likely that low-nominal-wage areas will reach the point where such adjustments are no longer sufficient at a lower federal minimum wage. The discussion here is limited to the initial imposition of a minimum wage in a fully covered economy. Similar differential impacts among regions apply to changes in the federal minimum-wage level.

FIGURE 14

SUPPLY AND DEMAND OF WORKER SKILLS, DETERMINATION OF
PRICE PER UNIT OF SKILL, AND SKILLS EMPLOYED FOR A NATIONAL
MINIMUM WAGE APPLIED UNIFORMLY IN HIGH- AND LOW-
COST-OF-LIVING REGIONS: NO WORKER FLOWS BETWEEN REGIONS

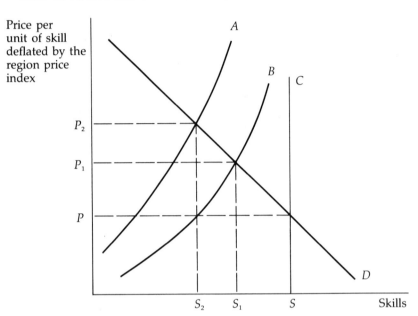

NOTE: Curve A is the supply of worker skills in the low-cost-of-living region in the presence of a national minimum wage of $\overline{W}$, from workers whose productivity is greater than the minimum wage. Curve B is the supply of worker skills in the high-cost-of-living region in the presence of a national minimum wage of $\overline{W}$, from workers whose productivity is greater than the minimum wage. Curve C is the supply of worker skills in each region in the absence of a minimum wage. Curve D is the demand for worker skills in each region. P is the price per unit of skill deflated by the region price deflator in the absence of a minimum wage. S is the quantity of skills employed in each region in the absence of a minimum wage. P_1 is the price per unit of skill in the high-cost-of-living region in the presence of the minimum wage. S_1 is the quantity of skills employed in the high-cost-of-living region in the presence of the minimum wage. P_2 is the price per unit of skill in the low-cost-of-living region in the presence of the national minimum wage. S_2 is the quantity of skills employed in the low-cost-of-living region in the presence of the minimum wage.

Just as worker flows among sectors in a single economy (discussed in chapter 3) reduced potential benefits to higher-skill workers, flows among regions reduce differential impacts on employment and earnings of workers. These flows suggest that medium-skill workers in low-wage areas (those disemployed in that region but employable in the high-wage area) will migrate to high-nominal-

FIGURE 15
EFFECT OF A NATIONAL MINIMUM WAGE ON WAGES AND EMPLOYMENT IN HIGH- AND LOW-COST-OF-LIVING REGIONS: FLOWS OF WORKERS BETWEEN REGIONS

A. High-cost-of-living-regions

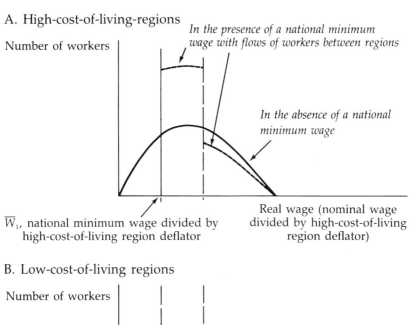

Number of workers

In the presence of a national minimum wage with flows of workers between regions

In the absence of a national minimum wage

$\overline{W}_1$, national minimum wage divided by high-cost-of-living region deflator

Real wage (nominal wage divided by high-cost-of-living region deflator)

B. Low-cost-of-living regions

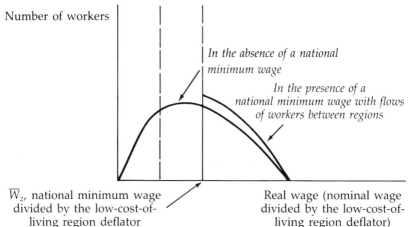

Number of workers

In the absence of a national minimum wage

In the presence of a national minimum wage with flows of workers between regions

$\overline{W}_2$, national minimum wage divided by the low-cost-of-living region deflator

Real wage (nominal wage divided by the low-cost-of-living region deflator)

wage areas and higher-skill workers will migrate to low-nominal-wage areas because of higher returns obtained there. This will continue until the ripple effect is equal among regions, the real wages of all those remaining employed being equated.

Figure 15 shows the manner in which flows of workers alter the skill composition of employment among regions. For simplicity the ripple effect is not depicted.[4] Workers in the low-wage region who would have earned less than $\overline{W}_2$, the real minimum wage in that region, but more than $\overline{W}_1$ flow to the high-wage area, while some higher-skill workers previously earning more than $\overline{W}_2$ migrate to the low-wage region. In both regions those earning less than $\overline{W}_1$ remain disemployed.

Once the minimum wage is imposed, further increases in its real level imply similar flows of workers among regions. The location of low-skill workers continually shifts to the high-nominal-wage region, however. Figure 16 depicts the process, the darkened lines representing the distribution of workers among regions with a real minimum wage of $\overline{W}_2$ and $\overline{W}_1$, exactly as shown in figure 15. A further increase in the national minimum wage increases the real minimum wage by more in the otherwise low-wage region, resulting in additional flows of medium-skill workers to the high-wage region.

Sufficiently large increases in the minimum mean that some workers in the low-wage region are disemployed and not employable in the high-wage region, those workers in the shaded portion of figure 16, part (B). In the absence of other incentives for migration, such as differential real welfare payments among regions, these people will most likely stay in their area. The brunt of more permanent disemployment occurs in the high-cost-of-living area, as given by the shaded area in part (A) of figure 16. Because the national minimum wage is an effectively different real minimum wage among areas, the distribution of medium-skill workers shifts to high-nominal-wage areas, where such workers are located when the minimum wage is again increased. The burden of local welfare payments then falls unequally among areas.[5]

Flows of Industry. As suggested by table 4, the location of manufacturing industries has altered the regional dispersion of economic activity. A characteristic of manufacturing industries is that they often form the base of a regional economy, with employment in other sectors (retail trade, wholesale trade, services, and so forth) induced by location of manufacturing industries. While direct im-

---

[4] The ripple effect would reduce the total number of disemployed but would still result in flows of high- and lower-skill workers.

[5] If future large increases in the minimum wage are expected, there is a decreased incentive for worker migration as depicted in figures 15 and 16. For small expected increases the higher-skilled of those migrating still have relatively large incentives to migrate, not all of them being disemployed because of small minimum-wage increases. In these circumstances more of the welfare burden is placed on areas with low cost-of-living levels.

FIGURE 16
EFFECT OF CHANGES IN A NATIONAL MINIMUM WAGE IN HIGH- AND LOW-COST-OF-LIVING REGIONS

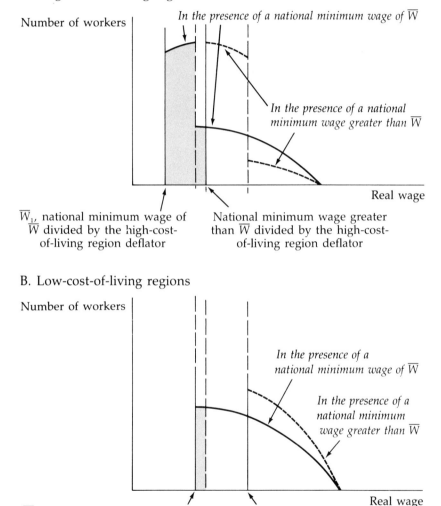

A. High-cost-of-living regions

Number of workers

In the presence of a national minimum wage of $\overline{W}$

In the presence of a national minimum wage greater than $\overline{W}$

Real wage

$\overline{W}_1$, national minimum wage of $\overline{W}$ divided by the high-cost-of-living region deflator

National minimum wage greater than $\overline{W}$ divided by the high-cost-of-living region deflator

B. Low-cost-of-living regions

Number of workers

In the presence of a national minimum wage of $\overline{W}$

In the presence of a national minimum wage greater than $\overline{W}$

Real wage

$\overline{W}_2$, national minimum wage of $\overline{W}$ divided by the low-cost-of-living region deflator

National minimum wage greater than $\overline{W}$ divided by the low-cost-of-living region deflator

NOTE: Shaded area represents the number of workers disemployed because of an increase in the national minimum wage.

51

pacts of the minimum wage on induced employment are likely to have less effect on location of employment of these industries, the impacts on location of basic manufacturing industries, for which location of production is less sensitive to location of output demand, could be substantial. Changes in the relative costs of labor induced through the ripple effect change the advantages associated with location of industry.[6] These effects are most likely longer term and depend on the extent to which worker flows, as shown in figure 15, do not in themselves allow for post-minimum-wage equalization of percentage changes in labor costs.

Summary

A national minimum wage applied uniformly among regions interacts with state-specific legislation to alter the extent and magnitude of minimum-wage restrictions on employment and worker compensation among states. Because people are mobile and can flow among regions within the United States, coverage of employment that is complete in one state while incomplete in other states leads to flows of workers among states, decreasing the impact of state-specific coverage on employment and earnings of workers. Because of differences among regions in costs of purchasing local goods and services and because of differences in amenity levels among regions, the nominal wage for a particular worker will differ, although the worker's well-being is equal among locations. The national minimum wage thus represents a different real minimum wage among regions, being higher in low-cost-of-living, high-amenity areas and lower in high-cost-of-living, low-amenity areas. In the presence of a national minimum wage, a particular worker located in a low-cost-of-living, high-amenity area may not be able to be employed there, while migration to another area with higher costs of living and/or lower amenity levels would lead to employability. The result is a concentration of lower-skill workers in areas such as many northeastern central cities, which, in the presence of increasing or fluctuating minimum wages, adds to the fiscal burdens of these areas.

[6] In terms of the discussion relating to figures 13 and 14, the demand curves in one region could shift to the other region when industry moves.

5

Empirical Findings

Implications for Empirical Modeling

The conceptual framework developed in chapters 3 and 4 implies that increases in the real minimum wage in a region raise the observed average wage in a covered industry in the first instance by disallowing employment of workers at wages below the minimum. In the absence of coverage in other sectors of the economy, these workers are merely replaced by higher-skill workers, with no change in the price per unit of skill. Increased coverage in other sectors leads to a limitation of such replacement flows and an increase in the price per unit of skill in the covered sector and reduced employment of skills. Workers remaining employed receive higher wages, which add to the observed average wage in already covered employment sectors of the economy. If the labor force is fixed, the average wage in the covered industry will increase as each worker previously employed and remaining employed receives a higher wage. Still, increased labor-force participation of other workers, induced into the labor market by the higher returns to market skills, makes the increase in the price per unit of skill less than would otherwise be the case. This tends to raise the observed average wage by less. If the new workers have skill levels less than the average of those previously working and remaining in the labor market, this would tend to reduce the increase in the average wage due to an increase in coverage, and possibly even reduce the observed average wage.

Differences in costs of living among regions mean that in the absence of worker flows among regions, percentage changes in the national minimum wage are greater percentage changes in the real minimum wage in low-cost-of-living areas than in high-cost-of-living areas, the difference being proportional to the relative costs of living. The average wage will be affected in proportion to these differences by a change in the national minimum wage. With worker flows between regions, percentage increases in the national minimum wage lead to flows of medium-skill workers to high-cost-of-living areas and high-skill workers to low-cost-of-living areas, with minimum-wage-induced increases in the average wage exacerbated in low-cost-of-living areas and mitigated or possibly even reversed in sign in high-cost-of-living areas. This suggests that the effect of a percentage change in the national minimum wage on the percentage change in the average wage in a covered industry is nonlinear in the regional cost of living, increasing as the cost of living decreases.

Empirical Modeling and Results

The data used in this study were compiled from U.S. Department of Labor average employment and earnings data by standard metropolitan statistical area (SMSA) for a variety of manufacturing industries from 1964 through 1975.[1] The focus of the empirical work is on the impacts of federal and state minimum-wage legislation, both coverage and minimum-wage levels, on the average wage in a particular industry for different SMSAs over time. Specifically, the percentage change in the average wage for a particular SMSA, industry, and time period, corrected for inflation, is modeled to depend on changes in minimum-wage coverage and level restrictions as well as other factors that would influence the average wage in the absence of minimum-wage legislation.

Effects of Minimum Wages. Table 6 presents estimates of the effect of a percentage change in the national minimum wage, corrected for inflation, on the percentage change in the average wage, corrected for inflation, by industry group. The estimates depend on the level of wages in a region that would exist in the absence of the minimum wage. The estimates are shown in table 6 for each industry category for the mean level of the regional deflator used to capture differences among regions in cost of living, amenity levels, and composition of worker skills, as well as for a region that would otherwise have average wages 25 percent greater than the norm and for a region that would have average wages 25 percent less than the norm.

For each industry group the results indicate that increases in the minimum wage increase the average hourly earnings of workers remaining employed. Moreover, these increases are greater in otherwise low-nominal-wage SMSAs, the effects sometimes increasing

---

[1] The empirical results reported here stem from the econometric model presented in appendix B. The estimates used stem from the results in table 11.

TABLE 6

Percentage Change in the Average Wage Due to a 1 Percent Change in the National Minimum Wage, by Industry

(coverage levels at their sample means)

Regional Deflator Level	Lumber and Products	Furniture and Fixtures	Stone, Clay, and Glass Products	Primary Metal Industries	Fabricated Metal Industries	Machinery except Electrical	Transportation Equipment	Food and Kindred Products	Apparel and Other Textile Products	Printing and Publishing	Chemicals and Petroleum
Sample mean average value of regional deflator	0.309	0.325	0.349	0.394	0.364	0.380	0.417	0.356	0.258	0.413	0.377
25 percent greater than the sample mean value	0.99	0.55	0.32	0.23	0.19	0.22	0.13	0.19	0.95	0.24	0.64
At sample mean value	1.59	0.86	0.45	0.30	0.20	0.34	0.18	0.31	1.48	0.36	0.99
25 percent less than the sample mean value	2.85	0.15	0.85	0.67	0.50	0.60	0.27	0.57	2.62	0.62	1.75

NOTE: Regional deflators are the nominal average wage in year $(t-1)$ divided by the U.S. consumer price index in period $(t-1)$ for each industry in each region.
SOURCE: Author; point estimates from table 11.

dramatically from the first row to the last row in table 6. The results differ by industry group, being greatest for lumber and wood products and apparel and other textile products. Of all the industries considered, these two had the lowest average wages in general, suggesting greater employment of lower-skill workers to begin with. The least affected industries are fabricated metal industries and transportation equipment, the latter having in general the highest average wages of all industry categories.

The results in table 6 indicate that increases in the average hourly wage induced by increases in the national minimum wage are greater for otherwise low-wage areas. The discussion in chapter 4 suggests that this is the case for two reasons. First, in the absence of worker flows among regions, a percentage change in the national minimum wage is a greater real change in the minimum in a low-wage area. Second, given this nonuniform change in the real minimum among regions resulting from a change in the national minimum wage, high-skill workers flow to the otherwise low-wage areas and lower-skill workers flow to the otherwise high-wage areas. Hence the percentage change in the average wage in an industry in an area due to a percentage change in the national minimum wage depends on the regional deflator level due to the first impact discussed above. Moreover, the effect of the regional deflator on this impact is in turn dependent on the regional deflator due to the second impact, the systematic flow of workers among regions.

Table 7 summarizes these two components of effects of regional deflators on percentage changes in the average wage in an industry due to a percentage change in the national minimum wage. Row (1) is the effect of a percentage change in the national minimum wage when the regional deflator is at its mean level among all SMSAs in the sample. Row (2) shows how a change in the regional deflator affects the estimates in row (1). Specifically, row (2) shows that the effect of a ten-cent decrease in the average wage in a region (in 1970 dollars) increases the sensitivity of average wage changes to changes in the national minimum wage. Row (3) shows the further effect of a ten-cent decrease in the regional deflator on the effect in row (2), capturing effects of flows of workers among regions. Estimates in both rows (2) and (3) are consistently positive: a decrease in the regional deflator increases effects of minimum wages on average wages at an increasing rate. These results indicate that flows of workers among regions in response to differential changes in real minimum wages induced by changes in the national minimum wage do take place. The results shown in table 6 are thus combinations of two effects: (1) the national minimum wage differs in real terms

TABLE 7

Effects of Regional Deflators on the Magnitude of Percentage Change in Average Wages Due to a 1 Percent Change in the National Minimum Wage, by Industry

	Lumber and Wood Products	Furniture and Fixtures	Stone, Clay, and Glass Products	Primary Metal Industries	Fabricated Metal Industries	Machinery except Electrical	Transportation Equipment	Food and Kindred Products	Apparel and Other Textile Products	Printing and Publishing	Chemicals and Petroleum
Sample mean average value of regional deflator	0.309	0.325	0.349	0.394	0.364	0.380	0.417	0.356	0.258	0.413	0.397
1. % change in average wage due to a 1% change in the national minimum wage—regional deflators at their means	1.59	0.86	0.45	0.30	0.20	0.34	0.18	0.31	1.48	0.36	0.99
2. Effect of a 10-cent change in the regional deflator on item 1	0.11	0.06	0.03	0.03	0.02	0.03	0.01	0.03	0.08	0.03	0.08
3. Effect of a 10-cent change in the regional deflator on item 2	0.03	0.02	0.01	0.01	0.01	0.01	0.00	0.01	0.02	0.01	0.03

NOTE: Regional deflators are the nominal average wage in year $(t-1)$ divided by the U.S. consumer price index in period $(t-1)$ for each industry in each region.
SOURCE: Author; point estimates from table 11.

by region, being higher in otherwise low-nominal-wage regions, and (2) because of these differentials low-skill workers flow to otherwise high-nominal-wage areas and high-skill workers flow to otherwise low-nominal-wage areas.

Effects of Coverage. Increased coverage of employment leads to an increased price per unit of skill, tending to increase average wages of those workers remaining employed. Because of enhanced labor market earnings, new workers flow into the labor market, affecting the skill composition of workers employed. Table 8 shows the effect of a one-unit increase in the percentage of employment covered in an SMSA on the percentage change in the average wage in an industry. All estimates are negative in sign. This means that the net impact of increased coverage incorporating both the ripple effect and increased labor-force participation of new workers leads to a decline in the observed average wage. The ripple effect of increased wage per worker is outweighed by an increase in medium-skill workers in the labor force, decreasing the average wage in the industry. Since the increased labor-force participation of new workers outweighs the increase in wage per worker through the ripple effect, the disemployment of very low skill workers is of major magnitude. These results indicate that the impact of increased coverage is to disemploy the lowest-skill workers, who are replaced by workers of somewhat higher skill who enter the labor market.

Summary

The empirical results strongly suggest that increased coverage of employment by minimum-wage legislation has served to decrease employment opportunities for low-skill workers. Increased coverage has served to increase labor costs for industries, but in response to the associated increase in the cost of worker skills, entry into the labor market of medium-skill workers is indicated. This implies that the ripple effect—the increase in returns to skill due to the minimum wage—is less than would otherwise be the case. Employment of low-skill workers is replaced by employment of new entrants into the labor market.

The national minimum wage, applied uniformly among regions that differ in cost-of-living levels, induces flows of workers between high- and low-cost-of-living areas. Some workers who would be disemployed in low-cost-of-living areas are able to gain employment in higher-cost-of-living regions. Moreover, high-skill workers living in high-cost-of-living areas are induced to flow to low-cost-of-living

TABLE 8

Percentage Change in Average Wages in an SMSA as a Result of an Increase in the Percentage of Employment Covered by Minimum-Wage Legislation, by Industry

	Lumber and Wood Products	Furniture and Fixtures	Stone, Clay, and Glass Products	Primary Metal Industries	Fabricated Metal Industries	Machinery except Electrical	Transportation Equipment	Food and Kindred Products	Apparel and Other Textile Products	Printing and Publishing	Chemicals and Petroleum
Percentage change in average wage as a result of increased coverage	−0.217	−0.069	−0.115	−0.027	−0.0014	−0.042	0.0007	−0.071	−0.078	−0.0001	−0.049

NOTE: The estimates presented here are the average of coverage increases in manufacturing and nonmanufacturing industry categories.
SOURCE: Table 12.

areas, replacing to some extent the loss of employment opportunities for low-skill workers in these areas. With coverage at present levels, however, the lowest-skill workers bear the brunt of the loss due to increases in the minimum wage, regardless of their location.

6

Summary and Policy Implications

Federal minimum-wage legislation has been applied nonuniformly among industries since its inception with the FLSA of 1938. In the presence of uneven coverage, impacts of the minimum wage on employment and earnings of workers are lessened because low-skill workers can be employed in uncovered industries. Since the early 1960s more and more types of employment opportunities have become subject to the national legislated wage floor. This trend has severely restricted the employment and earning opportunities of lower-skill workers in the market economy, not allowing for alternative sources of employment for these workers. Increases in the minimum wage under current coverage conditions lead to a replacement of lower-skill workers, who become disemployed as new workers enter the labor market.

The national minimum wage is applied uniformly to employment in covered industries among regions. Differences among regions in costs of purchasing goods and services and in amenities such as climate mean that in the absence of minimum-wage standards a worker of a given skill could earn a higher nominal wage in some regions and a lower nominal wage in others yet be just as well off in all locations. The national minimum wage is thus in effect a higher real minimum wage in those regions where workers would otherwise earn lower nominal wages. If workers could not migrate among regions, increases in the national minimum wage would represent greater real increases in the effective minimum wage in otherwise low-wage areas than in those where wages would be high. The result is a greater disemployment of workers and greater increase in labor cost in low-cost-of-living regions. Migration of workers reduces the regional disparity in employment and cost-of-labor impacts, however, because of unneccesary flows of low-skill workers to high-cost-of-living, low-amenity areas and flows of higher-skill workers to low-cost-of-living, high-amenity areas.

The intent of federal minimum-wage legislation has been to remedy alleged impacts of interstate commerce on the low standards of living of some workers. This suggests that the low standards of living of some workers in some areas can be maintained or exacerbated by producers who sell products across state lines. The assumption underlying this argument fails to take into account the mobility of labor itself. Large flows of population among regions in the United States in recent decades suggest that labor is mobile and in fact not totally subject to adverse working conditions in one area. Labor market conditions in one state, or even in one small community, are not determined independently of opportunities in other areas, and mobility of workers among regions not only allows for improvements in the quality of life but also serves as a check on employers' ability to exploit potential market power in any one location on the working conditions of their employees. The federal minimum wage itself imposes restrictions on the ability of workers and population to choose a desired location in which to live by setting unequal effective minimum-wage standards between locations.

The result that lower-skill workers may gain employment in high-cost-of-living, low-amenity areas, if anywhere, leads to a concentration of these workers in many of the central cities of the United States. Under such conditions the fiscal strain already burdening many of these areas is further complicated.

The prosperity of the U.S. economy and the welfare of the population depend critically on the efficient allocation of resources not only in each area of production activity but also among all possible locations. Labor plays an essential role in the production process. If the trend in increased minimum wages continues in future years, the growth and decline of economic activity among regions can be substantially altered. The minimum wage impairs the location decisions of employers and employees, thereby altering the allocation of resources among regions. Regions that offer high amenity levels and low costs of producing consumption goods and services will become high-cost-of-labor areas, driving industries to other areas. The national minimum wage in this context is a barrier to the workings of a competitive and efficient economy, burdening the current and future earning power of low-skill workers and distributing economic activity inappropriately among the states.

Appendix A
A General Approach for Examining Impacts of Minimum Wages

1. Approach

This appendix presents models for impacts of minimum wages on employment and compensation of workers that incorporate skill differences among workers and their ability to flow among industries and areas in order to avoid disemployment. The approach differs from those of other studies in that skill differences among workers in a particular job category are allowed, which explicitly determines who gains and who loses because of a minimum wage. The conceptual modeling provides the framework for estimation of the magnitudes involved and implications of empirical findings for policy evaluation.

Part 2 outlines a model for a single economy using labor skill distributions within an occupation to examine employment and compensation impacts of a completely binding minimum wage. It is shown that lower-skill workers unambiguously lose, while those who gain are higher-skill workers. The magnitudes of employment loss and compensation gains to those remaining employed are directly related to the increase in the price per unit of skill. Increased labor-force participation of higher-skill workers induced by increased labor market compensation results in greater disemployment of lower-skill workers and smaller increases in labor costs. Job rationing does not occur in this model. Worker skills determine who remains employed.

Part 3 extends the analysis to a multi-industry economy where some industries are not covered by minimum-wage legislation. Flows of workers among industries lead to the possibility of reduced impacts of a minimum wage on employment and earnings of all types of workers, with high-skill workers replacing low-skill workers in the covered industry and the latter flowing to the uncovered industry, replacing high-skill workers. At the extreme, while segmenting employment of workers of different skills, under costless mobility a minimum wage applied to a small enough section of the economy has no net impact on employment or compensation of workers. Increased coverage or a high enough minimum wage results in a breakdown of replacement options, leading to results similar to those in a fully covered economy.

Part 4 examines the implications of imposition of a uniform minimum wage among regions that differ in cost of living. The analysis would also be applicable to imposing different minimum wages among industries. As in the case of the covered/uncovered dichotomy, flows of workers introduce the possibility of lessened impacts on employment and compensation in low-cost-of-living areas. At high enough minimum-wage levels, differential changes in skill prices among areas provide incentives for movement of industry.

2. Full Coverage in a One-Industry Economy

Wage Determination with Skill Distributions. Let there be only one type of skill in the economy, so that there is only one job classification into which all workers fit. Ignoring other inputs besides labor in production, output depends on the level of effective labor skill services:

$$Q = g(X) \tag{1}$$

where Q is flow of output and X is a measure of effective labor skill services. Equation 1 implies that output depends, not on the number of laborers, but rather on the skill services provided by labor. If the rate of utilization is constant and the same for each laborer, only the composition of labor skills determines the measurement of X. If each laborer is allowed to possess a different amount of skill and these skills are perfect substitutes within this job category, X may be defined as

$$X = \sum_{i=1}^{N} \delta_i \tag{2}$$

where N is the number of workers and δ_i is the effective skill level of the ith laborer. Skill, as measured by δ_i, is determined by natural ability, education, on-the-job training, and the like. Although over

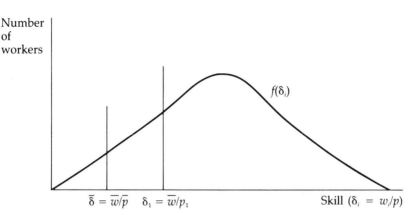

FIGURE 17
DISTRIBUTION OF WORKER SKILLS IN CONJUNCTION WITH
A MINIMUM WAGE

NOTE: The minimum wage, $\overline{w}$, is associated with a higher skill level for lower price per unit of skill, p.

time the skill level of a worker may change, at a point in time it may usefully be assumed that these δ_i terms are fixed.

To investigate more fully the effects of intra–job category skill differences among workers, let the set of δ_i be measured on $(0, 1)$, with δ_{max}, the highest skill load factor, normalized at unity. Further, let the price of laborers with skill level δ_{max} be p. With compensation for labor services limited to wage payments, the wage for the jth laborer is then $w_j = p\delta_j$. Under these assumptions, differences in wages among laborers are due only to differences in skill levels.

This distribution of effective skills in equation 2 is defined by the supply of workers of varying skill levels in the economy. Let $f(\delta_i)$ be the number of workers in the economy with skill level δ_i, so that total effective skill in the economy is

$$\int_0^1 \xi dF \, (\xi) \equiv H(0) \tag{3}$$

where F (ξ) is the total number of skills in the economy possessed by workers with ξ or less skill.

Figure 17 illustrates a skill distribution of workers which, given p, determines the wage distribution as well.

Industry demand for labor services is a function of the price of a normalized labor skill.

FIGURE 18
Determination of Price per Unit of Skill and Total Skills Employed from Demand and Supply of Worker Skills in an Economy with and without a Minimum Wage

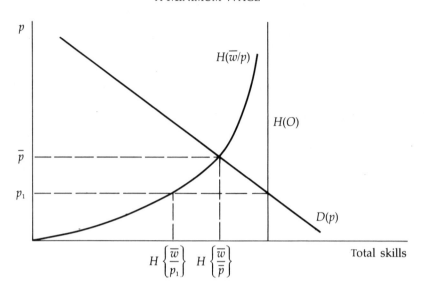

$$X = D(p) \tag{4}$$

Assuming full employment of all workers, the price of labor skill is determined by equating expressions 3 and 4. This is illustrated in figure 18, where $H(0)$ is the inelastic supply of worker skills given by equation 3. With no minimum wage, equilibrium skill price is p_1 and is determined by demand.

Suppose there is a fully binding minimum wage, $\overline{w}$, so that there is a δ, says $\overline{\delta} = \overline{w}/p$, such that workers with skill levels below $\overline{\delta}$ are not employed and workers with skills above $\overline{\delta}$ remain employed. The level of $\overline{\delta}$ depends on p for any given $\overline{w}$ and is shown in figure 17 as $\overline{\delta}_1 = \overline{w}/p_1$ for the pre-minimum-wage price of skill. Supply of skill above $\overline{\delta}$ as a function of p is shown in figure 18, with $H(\overline{\delta})$ $\equiv \int_{\overline{\delta}}^1 \xi dF\,(\xi)$. Increased p leads to decreased $\overline{w}/p$, which increases $H(\overline{\delta})$.

In equilibrium under the minimum-wage constraint

$$D(p) = H(\overline{\delta}) \tag{5}$$

which implies an equilibrium price, $\overline{p}$, associated with $\overline{w}$. Substituting $\overline{w}/\overline{p} = \overline{\delta}$ in equation 5, totally differentiating, and rearranging gives

$$(d\bar{p}/d\bar{w}) = [H'(\bar{w}/\bar{p})\,(1/\bar{p})]/[D'(\bar{p}) + H'(\bar{w}/\bar{p})\,(\bar{w}/\bar{p}^2)] \qquad (6)$$

The term in the numerator measures changes in the amount of labor skill below $\bar{\delta}$ if $\bar{w}$ is increased. The denominator captures the combined impact of changes in p on quantity demanded and the amount of labor skill below $\bar{\delta}$.

Since $D'(\cdot)$ and $H'(\cdot)$ are both negative, $d\bar{p}/d\bar{w} > 0$, so that increases in the minimum wage unambiguously increase the wages of those remaining employed. This relationship is depicted graphically in figure 18.

A perfectly elastic demand curve at p_1 would result in a decrease in employment in figure 18 from $H(O)$ to $H(\bar{w}/\bar{p}_1)$, while a noninfinite elasticity of labor skill demand implies that the price of an effective labor skill unit increases because of increases in the minimum wage, reducing the labor skill employment impact to $[H(O) - H(\bar{w}/\bar{p})]$, with $\bar{p} > p_1$. The ripple effect is captured by the difference between these two measures, $H(\bar{w}/\bar{p}) - H(\bar{w}/\bar{p}_1)$, and is induced by the increase in $\bar{p}$ due to an increase in $\bar{w}$, which initiates the first-order disemployment effects of a wage minimum. Further increases in $\bar{w}$ shift $H(\bar{w}/\bar{p})$ to the left in figure 18, increasing equilibrium $\bar{p}$ and decreasing employment of effective skills in the economy.

This model implies that the benefits of increases in the minimum wage are only for those high-skill workers who remain employed with higher compensation than before. Low-skill workers are unambiguously worse off, being disemployed. Arbitrary job rationing does not occur in this model, differences in worker skills determining who remains employed.

Dividing equation 6 by the equilibrium quantity of effective labor services employed and rearranging yields

$$(\dot{\bar{p}}/\dot{\bar{w}}) = 1/[1 + (\eta/\varepsilon)] \qquad (7)$$

where $\dot{\bar{p}}$ is the percentage change in $\bar{p}$, $\dot{\bar{w}}$ is the percentage change in $\bar{w}$, $\eta = [\bar{p}D'\,(\bar{p})]/X$ is the elasticity of demand, and $\varepsilon = [H'(\bar{w}/\bar{p})w]/[H(\bar{w}/\bar{p})\bar{p}]$ is the elasticity of effective labor supply with respect to changes in skill level. Given η and ε, the change in the price of a labor skill unit with changes in the minimum wage is determined.

The example above considers one job category within which all skill levels are perfect substitutes. A more general analysis of employment of effective labor skills is needed when laborers serve different functions in the production process. Each function may then be considered a separate job category (input) in the production function. Let there be n job categories in the economy $(X_1, X_2, \ldots, X_n)$, with production depending on the level of total labor skill services in each job classification. The demand for skills of the ith type is given by

$$X_i = D_i(p_1, p_2, \ldots, p_n) \qquad i = 1, \ldots, n \qquad (8)$$

where p_i is the price of a unit of skill in the ith job category. The supply of effective skill in job category i is assumed to be of the form given in equation 3 for each job category, with mutual exclusivity between job classifications:

$$\int_0^1 \xi dF_i(\xi) \qquad i = 1, \ldots, n \qquad (9)$$

where $F_i (\xi)$ is the skill supply function for the ith job category.

Effects of changes in the minimum wage applied equally to each job category on the price of a skill unit in each job category result from the solution of

$$
\begin{bmatrix}
\eta_{11} - \varepsilon_1 & \eta_{12} & \ldots \eta_{1n} \\
\eta_{21} & \eta_{22} - \varepsilon_2 & \ldots \eta_{2n} \\
\cdot & \cdot & \\
\cdot & & \cdot \\
\cdot & & \cdot \\
\eta_{n1} & \eta_{n2} & \eta_{nn} - \varepsilon_n
\end{bmatrix}
\begin{bmatrix}
\dot{\overline{p}}_1 \\
\dot{\overline{p}}_2 \\
\cdot \\
\cdot \\
\cdot \\
\dot{\overline{p}}_n
\end{bmatrix}
=
\begin{bmatrix}
\dot{\overline{w}}\varepsilon_1 \\
\dot{\overline{w}}\varepsilon_2 \\
\cdot \\
\cdot \\
\cdot \\
\dot{\overline{w}}\varepsilon_n
\end{bmatrix}
\qquad (10)
$$

where ε_i is the elasticity of effective labor supply with respect to skill level for the ith job category and η_{ij} is the elasticity of demand of effective labor skills of job category i with respect to a change in the jth job category's unit skill price. Interaction among demand for skill types with respect to prices of skill types means that the solution in (7) for a particular skill category is inadequate under some situations. For example, let there be only two job categories, with a change in the minimum wage applicable to both. Then

$$\dot{\overline{p}}_1/\dot{\overline{w}} = [\varepsilon_1(\eta_{22} - \varepsilon_2) - \varepsilon_2\eta_{12}]/[(\eta_{11} - \varepsilon_1)(\eta_{22} - \varepsilon_2) - \eta_{12}\eta_{21}] \quad (11)$$

which simplifies to $\varepsilon_1/(\eta_{11} - \varepsilon_1)$ if there is no demand interaction, $\eta_{12} = \eta_{21} = 0$. Further, if the minimum wage is applicable only to the first job category,

$$\dot{\overline{p}}_1/\dot{\overline{w}} = \varepsilon_1(\eta_{22} - \varepsilon_2)/D \text{ and } \dot{\overline{p}}_2/\dot{\overline{w}} = -\eta_{21}\varepsilon_1/D$$

where D is the denominator on the right-hand side of (11).

Substitution and complementarity between job functions allow for increases in the minimum wage (applicable to some or all job categories) to be less or more effective in increasing the prices of different job skill units, thereby affecting the extent of ripple effects

68

and the resulting employment impacts of the minimum wage. Capital services could be considered one of the inputs and thereby integrated into the model, with no minimum wage applied to that input. For labor in any particular job category, however, the lowest-skill workers are those who stand to lose, although the skill level that separates gainers and losers, and hence the magnitude of effects, are affected by impacts of minimum wages on other input prices.

Price Elasticity of Effective Labor Supply. The model developed above assumes that the supply of labor skills in the economy is perfectly inelastic with respect to compensation received. Movement in and out of the labor force suggests that this is not the case and is vital for analyzing the impact of the minimum wage not only on employment but also on activities related to nonwork conditions (such as welfare).

Let the supply of effective labor services depend on the price of a normalized effective labor skill, with the number of workers with a given skill level increasing as p increases.

In equilibrium,

$$D(\bar{p}) = \int_{\underline{\delta}}^{1} \xi \, dF(\xi, \bar{p}) = H(\bar{\delta}, \bar{p})$$

Differentiating and rearranging gives

$$\bar{p}/\bar{w} = 1/[1 + \eta/\varepsilon - \theta/\varepsilon] \qquad (12)$$

where $\theta = [H_2(\bar{w}/\bar{p},\bar{p})p]/[H(\bar{w}/\bar{p},\bar{p})]$ is the price elasticity of supply of effective labor skill. If θ is large, so that the distribution of effective labor supply shifts out as p goes up, there will be less effect of changes in the minimum wage on $\bar{p}$. In the extreme case where $\theta = \infty$, there is no effect at all.

In the example above, since more high-skill labor enters the labor force as the return to skills increases, the ripple effect is reduced, with $\bar{p}$ changing less than otherwise. High-skill labor receives all the benefits of a minimum wage, although each worker remaining employed does not receive as much as in the case of a fixed labor force. Some of the benefits accrue to newly employed high-skill workers. With workers possessing multiple job skills, the effective skill supply for a particular job category would depend on the whole set of p_j, with changes in p_j for supply of X_i including job-switch responses. This would involve inclusion of ε_{ij} terms on the off-diagonal elements in expression (10) but does not greatly alter the implications of the model.

3. Multi-Industry Analysis

The national minimum wage is applied differently among industries and often between firms within an industry. Coverage is thereby an important potential influence on the direction and magnitude of employment effects of the minimum wage in different industries.

Consider an economy consisting of two industries, the first covered, the second uncovered, serving as an alternative means of employment for low-skill workers disemployed in the covered industry as the minimum wage increases. Assume one job category in the economy, with industry demands for labor

$$X_1 = D_1(p_1)$$
$$X_2 = D_2(p_2)$$

where p_1 and p_2 are the prices of an effective skill unit in each industry. When both markets clear, $p_1 = p_2 = p$, with demand for labor equal to supply.

$$X = D_1(p) + D_2(p) = \int_0^1 \xi dF(\xi)$$

where for simplicity supply is assumed to be perfectly price-inelastic.

In the case considered above, there is no specification of how laborers sort themselves between industries to start with, so that the effect of changes in employment of effective skill services cannot be mapped into changes in employment of workers without further specification of how the total distribution of effective labor skills is split among industries. Industry-specific skill factors could be introduced in the skill distribution function to effect an interindustry sorting of skills. In the absence of systematic differences in incentives to hire low- or high-skill workers of a particular job category among firms, however, with many firms in an industry (and/or many personnel officers within a firm), the distribution of skills for a particular job category will be similar among industries. Data on wage distributions for particular job categories among industries are consistent with this assumption.

Differences in coverage among industries will affect this sorting mechanism and the resulting distribution of employment and the price of skill services. Since employers are assumed to be indifferent as to composition of the skill distribution of workers, it is possible that imposition of a minimum wage in one industry merely results in a flow of higher-skill laborers from the uncovered to the covered sector without any change in the wages of an employee at a given skill level.

Let the initial distribution of skill levels employed by each industry be of the same form, with the first industry employing α of the total effective labor skills and the second industry employing the remainder $(1 - \alpha)$. If

$$\int_{\delta}^{1} \xi dF(\xi) \leq D_1(p^{\circ}) = \alpha \int_{0}^{1} \xi dF(\xi) \qquad (13)$$

where p° is the equilibrium price of labor with skill level δ_{max} before the imposition of the minimum wage, then sorting could be accomplished, after which all workers are employed at their previous wage after the minimum is introduced. If the quantity demanded of effective labor skills in the covered industry prior to imposition of the minimum-wage constraint is less than the supply above that level at which the minimum wage truncates the total labor skill supply as in expression (13), workers could be rearranged among industries, with no net disemployment resulting and no change in the wage for a worker at any skill level. This is illustrated in figure 19, with pre-minimum-wage worker skill distributions given by $\alpha f(\delta)$ in the covered sector and $(1 - \alpha)f(\delta)$ in the uncovered sector. A minimum wage of $\overline{w}$ implies a skill level of $\overline{\delta}$ for given p. Workers with $(\delta < \overline{\delta})$ could flow out of the covered into the uncovered sector, replaced by flows of some workers with $(\delta > \overline{\delta})$ out of the uncovered into the covered sector. The resulting worker skill distributions are given by the dashed lines in figure 19, and no change in equilibrium p need take place to induce this sorting. When the inequality in expression 13 holds, skill price is determined as in figure 18, where the relevant demand is aggregate demand. The mechanism by which such a transfer of labor between industries is made, however, could be quite important in determining the final distribution of labor skills among industries, with positive costs of changing jobs entering as an important qualification.

If the inequality in expression 13 does not hold, there will be changes in the price of effective labor skills, with wages in the covered sector for a given skill level increasing and those in the uncovered sector decreasing. In terms of figure 19 this is the case when the minimum wage exceeds that level at which all workers with $(\delta > \overline{\delta})$ have already flowed into the covered sector, with no overlapping of skill levels among the two sectors. Now, supply of these workers in the economy becomes a constraint for the covered sector, with skill price in the covered sector determined as in figure 18 except

71

FIGURE 19
EFFECT OF A MINIMUM WAGE APPLIED IN ONLY ONE INDUSTRY THAT IN THE ABSENCE OF A MINIMUM WAGE EMPLOYS ONLY SOME OF THE TOTAL SKILLS IN THE ECONOMY

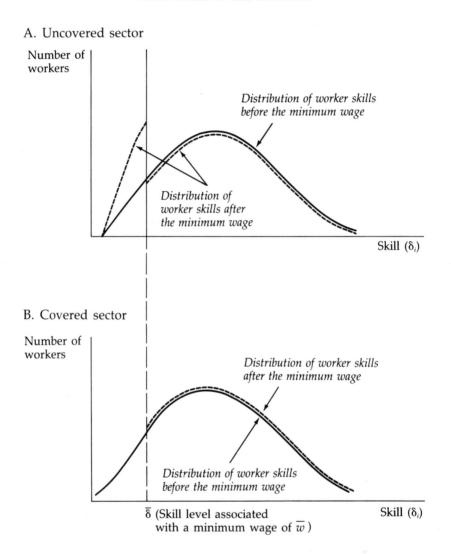

A. Uncovered sector

Number of workers

Distribution of worker skills before the minimum wage

Distribution of worker skills after the minimum wage

Skill (δ_i)

B. Covered sector

Number of workers

Distribution of worker skills after the minimum wage

Distribution of worker skills before the minimum wage

$\bar{\delta}$ (Skill level associated with a minimum wage of $\bar{w}$)

Skill (δ_i)

NOTE: Such application of a minimum wage leads to flows of low-skill workers to the uncovered industry and their replacement by higher-skill workers who flow to the covered industry. No change in individual worker wages occurs.

72

that the relevant demand curve is the covered sector demand. $H(O)$ for the covered sector relates to that δ which results in equality in expression 13. In equilibrium there will be no net disemployment, with

$$D_1(\bar{p}_1) = \int_{\delta}^{1} \xi dF(\xi) = H_1(\bar{w}/\bar{p}_1) \qquad (14)$$

$$D_2(\bar{p}_2) = \int_{0}^{\delta} \xi dF(\xi) = H(0) - H_1(\bar{w}/\bar{p}_1) \qquad (15)$$

where $\bar{\delta} = (\bar{w}/\bar{p}_1)$. Increasing the minimum wage will increase the price of an effective skill unit for those high-skill laborers employed in the first industry in expression 14 while decreasing it for low-skill workers employed in the uncovered industry in expression 15.

Differentiating expression 14 results in an expression similar to equation 7.

$$\frac{dp_1}{d\bar{w}} = [H_1' (w/p_1) \frac{1}{p_1}]/[D_1'(p_1) + H_1' (w/p_1)\frac{w_2}{p_1}] \qquad (16)$$

As before, $d\bar{p}_1/d\bar{w} > 0$, so that those workers remaining employed in the covered industry after increases in the minimum wage are better off. On the other hand, differentiating (15) yields

$$[D_2'(p_2)]\frac{dp_2}{dw} = [H_1'(w/p_1)\frac{w_2}{p_1}\frac{d_{p_1}}{d\bar{w}} - H_1'\frac{\bar{w}}{p_1^2}] \qquad (17)$$

The term in brackets on the left-hand side of the expression above is negative, while the terms in the brackets on the right-hand side are opposite in sign. The first term represents the effect of an increase in p_1, which acts to reduce the effectiveness of the minimum wage due to a ripple effect, while the second term represents the direct effect of increasing $\bar{w}$. Rearranging and substituting from expression 7, the right-hand side becomes

$$H_1'(\bar{w}/p_1) \frac{1}{p_1} \left[\frac{\eta_1/\varepsilon}{1 + \eta_1/\varepsilon} \right]$$

where η_1 is the elasticity of demand for effective skill services in the first industry. The term in brackets is positive (stemming from the net increase in $\bar{\delta}$ due to increases in the minimum wage) so that

$$\frac{d\bar{p}_2}{d\bar{w}} = \frac{1}{p_1} H_1'[(\eta_1/\varepsilon)/(1 + \eta_1/\varepsilon)]/D_2'(p_2)$$

is negative. While all workers remain employed in this model, those

73

with low skills are employed in the uncovered sector and are un-ambiguously worse off with

$$\dot{p}_2/\dot{w} = - (\eta_1/\eta_2)/(1 + \eta_1/\varepsilon)$$

Hence the greater the elasticity of demand in the second (uncovered) industry, the smaller the reduction in compensation for the lower-skill workers employed there.

With positive elasticities of worker skill supply, higher-skill workers will be induced into the labor market, tending to reduce the ripple effect, while lower-skill workers will flow out of the labor force, tending to increase the ripple effect. The net impact on the change in p of entry and exit from the labor market depends on the skill-weighted supply elasticities of workers with different skill levels.

4. Multiregion Analysis

The national minimum wage, in the absence of coverage differentials among regions, is applied uniformly to all areas of the United States. If nominal wage levels among areas differ in the absence of such legislation, the nominal national minimum wage is an effectively higher real minimum in otherwise low-wage regions. With flows of workers (and industries) among areas, differential regional impacts of federal minimum-wage legislation may be usefully examined in terms of sectors (industries) facing different real-minimum-wage levels.

Let the supply of effective skill services be perfectly inelastic with respect to the price of a skill unit. Let the minimum wage be $\overline{w}_1$ for the first industry and $\overline{w}_2$ for the second industry, with $\overline{w}_1 > \overline{w}_2$. Under these conditions there will be some workers disemployed, those affected by the lowest minimum wage, $\overline{w}_2$, while other workers will be affected through changes in compensation.

Consider the case where only the first industry faces a minimum wage such that the inequality in expression 13 holds for $\overline{\delta} = \overline{w}_1/p_1$, so that regardless of the distribution of skills among the two indus-tries, it is possible that the first industry can employ the same level of skill services as before this minimum was introduced. With no minimum in the second industry, all workers would remain em-ployed, with no change in compensation for a particular skill level. This is analogous to the covered/uncovered dichotomy discussed in part 3. A minimum wage in the second industry that is lower than that in the first industry means those workers with $\overline{\delta} < \overline{\delta}_2$ are not employable in that sector. Still, the increase in p_2 resulting from the ripple effect in the second industry means that higher-skill workers will find employment in the second industry advantageous, flowing out of the first industry, with the price of skills increasing there until equal pay for a given skill level in each industry is attained. This is illustrated in figure 20, where, for illustrative purposes, the ripple effect is not shown. Workers with $\delta_1 < \delta < \delta_2$ who were previously employed in the first sector could obtain employment at the same wage in the second sector, replaced by workers with $\delta > \delta_2$ who were previously employed in the second sector. The dashed curves in figure 20 show the resulting distribution of worker skills among sectors.

When the constraint in expression 13 is not binding, the compensation of high-skill laborers is not affected by $\overline{w}_1$, with

$$D_1(p_1) + D_2(p_2) = \int_{\delta_2}^{1} \xi dF(\xi)$$

and $p_1 = p_2 = p$. In this case $\overline{w}_2/\overline{p}_2 = \overline{w}_2/p$. The restriction on supply of higher-skill workers determined by $\overline{w}_1$ is not effective, so that all workers remaining employed in both industries benefit from increases in $\overline{w}_2$.

In the case above, if workers can migrate costlessly, there is no incentive for firms to move. Instead, a regional shift in skill characteristics results, with higher-skill workers moving to the area with the high minimum-wage constraint (low-wage areas) and lower-skill workers moving to the low-minimum-wage region.

When the inequality in expression 13 does not hold, all high-skill workers will be employed in the first industry, with the rest employed in the second industry. In terms of figure 20 this is the case when $\overline{w}_1/p$ is so high that there is no overlapping of skill levels among sectors, with the dashed line in figure 20 on the axis. It is in this situation that the analogy between regions and industries within a region facing different minimum wages is altered. Industries producing goods for a national market may choose different locations because of relative input price differences. Changes in labor costs could induce switching among regions, and the dichotomy between $D_1(\cdot)$ and $D_2(\cdot)$ is no longer appropriate. Still, a good deal of production (especially services) is location-specific, and the analogy is useful for analyzing these industries. A qualification is that switching of manufacturing industries among regions due to differential minimum wages may lead to changes in demand for region-specific consumption goods. When expression 13 is not satisfied, increases in $\overline{w}_2$ serve to increase the price of all high-skill workers, shifting

FIGURE 20
Effect of a National Minimum Wage in the Presence of Equilibrium Cost-of-Living Differences among Regions

A. First sector (low nominal wage)

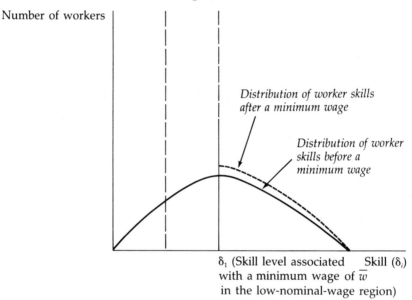

Number of workers

Distribution of worker skills after a minimum wage

Distribution of worker skills before a minimum wage

δ_1 (Skill level associated with a minimum wage of $\overline{w}$ in the low-nominal-wage region)   Skill (δ_i)

B. Second sector (high nominal wage)

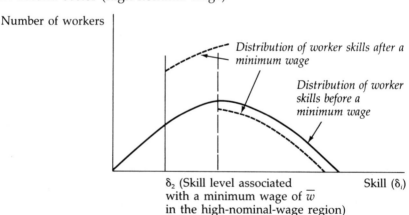

Number of workers

Distribution of worker skills after a minimum wage

Distribution of worker skills before a minimum wage

δ_2 (Skill level associated with a minimum wage of $\overline{w}$ in the high-nominal-wage region)   Skill (δ_i)

NOTE: A uniform minimum wage applied under these circumstances results in flows of medium-skill workers to the high-cost-of-living region and flows of high-skill workers to the low-cost-of-living region, with disemployment of the lowest-skill workers.

76

some of the high-skill workers out of the first industry (increasing the price of an effective skill unit). If $p_2 > p_1$, then the high-skill workers would not work in the first industry. Because of the inequality in expression 13, $p_1 \geq p_2$, with equality holding only for equality in expression 13, as illustrated earlier in this section. Then $\overline{w}_1/p_1 > \overline{w}_1/p_2$, so that the lower bound on skills employed in the first industry is $\overline{w}_1 p_1$, which is also the upper bound for skills in the second industry. Although both $\overline{w}_1 > \overline{w}_2$ and $\overline{p}_1 > \overline{p}_2$, the effective skill level that provides a lower bound for employment in the first industry is higher than that for the second industry, $\delta_1 > \delta_2$.

In equilibrium, with minimum wages in both industries:

$$D_1(p_1) = \int_{\overline{w}_1/p_1}^{1} \xi dF(\xi) \equiv H(\overline{w}_1/p_1) \tag{18}$$

$$D_2(p_2) = \int_{\overline{w}_2/p_2}^{\overline{w}_1/p_1} \xi dF(\xi) \equiv H(\overline{w}_2/p_2) - H(\overline{w}_1/p_1) \tag{19}$$

In expression 18 employment in the first industry consists of only those workers with skills greater than or equal to $\delta_1 = \overline{w}_1/p_1$, while employment in the second industry consists of those with skills such that $\delta_1 = \overline{w}_1/p_1 \geq \delta_2 = \overline{w}_2/p_2$. Those workers with skills less than δ_1 are not employed, while the compensation for workers employed depends on which industry they are employed in as well as on their skill level.

Differentiating these equilibrium relationships first with respect to a change in $\overline{w}_1$ yields

$$\frac{d\overline{p}_1}{d\overline{w}_1} = [H'(\overline{w}_1/\overline{p}_1)\frac{1}{p}]/[D_1'(\overline{p}_1) + H'(\overline{w}_1/\overline{p}_1)\frac{\overline{w}_1}{\overline{p}_1^2}] \tag{20}$$

$$\frac{d\overline{p}_2}{d\overline{w}_1} = \left[-H'(\overline{w}_1/\overline{p}_1)\frac{1}{\overline{p}_1} + H'(\overline{w}_1/\overline{p}_1)\frac{(\overline{w}_1)}{\overline{p}_1^2}\frac{d\overline{p}_1}{d\overline{w}_1} \right]/\left[D_2'(\overline{p}_2) \right.$$

$$\left. + H'\frac{(\overline{w}_2)\overline{w}_2}{\overline{p}_2\overline{p}_2^2} \right] \tag{21}$$

The expression in equation 20 is positive, so that, as before, increases in the minimum wage in the first sector increase the compensation of those remaining employed while decreasing the number employed. The expression in equation 21 combines the effect of the change in the value of the upper bound in the integral in equation 19 with the effects of this change on $\overline{p}_2$. Substituting expression 20 in expression 21 yields

$$\frac{d\bar{p}_2}{dw_1} = \left[-D_1'(\bar{p}_1)H'(\bar{w}_1)\frac{1}{\bar{p}_1} \right] \Bigg/ \left[\left(D_1'(\bar{p}_1) + H'\frac{(\bar{w}_1)}{\bar{p}_1}\frac{\bar{w}_1}{\bar{p}_1^2} \right) \left(D_2'(p_2) \right) \right.$$

$$\left. + H'\frac{(\bar{w}_2)}{\bar{p}_2}\frac{\bar{w}_2}{\bar{p}_2^2} \right) \right]$$

Both terms in the denominator are negative, so that $d\bar{p}_2/d\bar{w}$ is unambiguously negative. From expression 21, although the initial increase in w_1/p_1 due to an increase in w_1 is offset somewhat by the increase in p_1 from expression 20, the net result is an increase in w_1/p_1, serving to drive p_2 down. This decrease is not offset by the increase in w_2/p_2, which is captured in the denominator of expression 21, since the increase in the lower bound of the integral in expression 19 stems only from a net decrease in p_2 due to the interindustry effects captured by the numerator.

Hence an increase in the minimum wage for the first industry decreases employment in that industry while increasing it in the second industry. Still, the decreased price of an effective skill unit in the second industry increases $\bar{w}_2/\bar{p}_2$, so that more workers are disemployed on net from such a change in the minimum-wage structure. The increase in employment of skill services in the second industry is a combination of a flow of labor skills from the first to the second industry and a flow of lower-skill workers out of the second industry, the former being larger in magnitude. The opposite directions of change of $\bar{p}_1$ and $\bar{p}_2$ serve to increase the differential $\bar{p}_1 - \bar{p}_2$.

The effect of a change in $\bar{w}_2$ is quite different from that of a change in $\bar{w}_1$. Differentiating the equilibrium relationships in expressions 18 and 19 yields

$$\frac{d\bar{p}_1}{d\bar{w}_2} = 0 \tag{22}$$

$$\frac{d\bar{p}_2}{d\bar{w}_2} = \left[H'\ (\bar{w}_2\bar{p}_2)\frac{1}{\bar{p}_2} \right] \Bigg/ \left[D_2'(\bar{p}_2) + H'(\bar{w}_2/\bar{p}_2)\frac{\bar{w}_2}{\bar{p}_2^2} \right] \tag{23}$$

The effect of a change in $\bar{w}_2$ on $\bar{p}_1$ is zero, while the increase in $\bar{p}_2$ is positive and similar to that in expression 6. Essentially, the initial price differential, $\bar{p}_1 - \bar{p}_2 > 0$, implies that a change in $\bar{w}_2$ will not affect employment or compensation in the first industry because $\bar{w}_2$ is not an effective constraint on the labor skill levels employed. Hence $\bar{w}_1/\bar{p}_1$ is parametric to both industries for a change in $\bar{w}_2$. The result is that changes in the lower minimum wage will only affect that industry's employment and compensation characteristics. Since $\bar{p}_2$ increases, however, the price differential is decreased, with equality resulting only when $\bar{w}_1 = \bar{w}_2$.

Appendix B
Empirical Modeling and Results

1. Implications of the Conceptual Framework for Empirical Modeling

The conceptual framework developed in appendix A implies that an increase in the real minimum wage in a region leads to a higher observed average wage in a covered industry in the first instance by disallowing employment of workers at wages below the minimum. In the absence of coverage in other sectors of the economy, these workers are merely replaced by higher-skill workers with no change in the price per unit of skill. Increased coverage in other sectors leads to a limitation of such replacement flows and increase in the price per unit of skill in the covered sector and reduced employment of skills. If the labor force is fixed, the average wage in the covered industry will increase as each worker remaining employed receives a higher wage. Still, increased labor-force participation of other workers, induced into the labor market by the higher returns to market skills, makes the increase in the price per unit of skill smaller than would otherwise be the case and, if these new workers are of medium-skill level, could decrease the observed average wage.

Differences in costs of living among regions mean that in the absence of worker flows among regions, percentage changes in the national minimum wage are greater percentage changes in the real minimum wage in low-cost-of-living areas than in high-cost-of-living areas, the difference being proportional to the relative costs of living. The average wage will be affected in proportion to these differences by a change in the national minimum wage. With worker flows between regions, percentage increases in the national minimum wage lead to flows of medium-skill workers to high-cost-of-living areas and high-skill workers to low-cost-of-living areas, with minimum-wage-induced increases in the average wage exacerbated in low-cost-of-living areas and mitigated (and possibly even reversed in sign) in high-cost-of-living areas. This suggests that the effect of a percentage change in the national minimum wage on the percentage change in the average wage in a covered industry is nonlinear in the regional cost of living, increasing as the cost of living decreases.

Besides different effects of changes in coverage and the real minimum wage on the average wage in an industry in a region and the nonlinear effects of cost-of-living differences, because of flows of workers among regions, national changes in worker productivity over time and changes in regional cost-of-living levels affect the time patterns of average wage behavior. In addition, national fluctuations in economic activity lead to shifts in manufacturing industry demand for labor, which affects the average wage in the presence of regional labor supply functions that are not perfectly elastic in the short run. In this appendix, the variables constructed to capture these factors are discussed, and estimates of their impacts on average wages are presented.

2. Data Employed and Variable Definitions

The empirical work focuses on the percentage change in the average wage, corrected for national inflation, for a particular manufacturing industry, region, and time period as it is affected by minimum-wage legislation. The data used are compiled from U.S. Department of Labor average yearly employment and earnings data by SMSA for a variety of manufacturing industries from 1964 through 1975. Minimum-wage and coverage changes are known sufficiently far in advance to make yearly employment and earnings averages useful in capturing shifts in skill structures implied by the model. Migration flows of people among areas are also sufficient to suggest that effects of minimum wages on these flows can be captured by yearly average data. The cost of adjustment suggests that some adjustment to changes in minimum-wage legislation takes place before the legislation becomes effective as well as for a time after new legislation is imposed. If these adjustment times are short, yearly average earnings data can still lead to useful insights into the nature of equilibrium changes in the composition of worker skill employment.

A nominal minimum wage differs in real terms over time because of inflation and among areas at any point in time because of differences in regional price levels. The real minimum wage in the jth area in period t is

$$RMW_{jt} = \frac{NMW_{jt}}{\pi_t \delta_{jt}}$$

where NMW_{jt} is the nominal-minimum-wage level in the jth area in period t, π_t is the U.S. consumer price index, and δ_{jt} is a region-specific adjustment to π_t.

Productivity Growth and Regional Cost of Living in the Absence of Minimum Wages. For a particular industry, let $DRAW_{jt}$ be the percentage change in the real average wage in the jth SMSA.[1] In a steadily growing or declining region in the absence of a minimum wage, the only factors influencing $DRAW_{jt}$ would be the rate of productivity increase or change in composition of jobs (possibly as a result of technological change) and change over time in region-specific price deflators:

$$DRAW_{jt} = \rho_t + r_{jt}$$

where ρ_t is the rate of worker productivity increase and r_{jt} is the rate of change in δ_{jt}. For empirical purposes it is assumed that $\rho_t = \rho$ and $r_{jt} = r_j$.

Changes in the Real Minimum Wage. Ignoring flows of workers among regions, changes in the national minimum wage over time affect the level at which the wage distribution is intersected by the minimum wage and hence by the observed average wage. With the real national minimum wage $RNMW_{jt} = NMW_{jt}/\pi_t$, a percentage change in $RNMW_{jt}$ implies a percentage change in the real regional minimum of

$$\frac{DRNMW_{jt}}{\delta_{jt}} \tag{24}$$

in the absence of productivity growth. At any point in time cumulative changes in productivity serve to shift the real minimum wage relative to the wage distribution in a manner similar to the cumulative change in r_j up to that time.

To capture the impacts of changes in δ_{jt} adequately, both over time and among regions in conjunction with increased worker productivity, consider deflating $DRNMW_{jt}$ by RAW_{jt-1}:

$$DRMW_{jt} = \frac{DRNMW_{jt}}{RAW_{jt-1}} \tag{25}$$

[1] This variable has been corrected for variation in overtime hours worked.

Changes in RAW_{jt-1} over time capture productivity trends as well as region-specific price deflator growth, and differences in RAW_{jt-1} among regions at any point in time capture variation in region-specific price deflator levels. Past-period, cumulative impacts of the minimum wage on the worker skill distribution are also reflected by RAW_{jt-1}.

With flows of workers among regions due to differential increases in real regional minimum-wage levels resulting from a uniform increase in the federal minimum, it is expected that average real wages in low-cost-of-living regions will increase by more than those in high-cost-of-living regions. The extent to which flows of workers exacerbate or mitigate increased real average wages because of increases in the national minimum wage depends on the cost-of-living deflator. Multiplying expression 25 by $1/RAW_{jt-1}$, gives

$$DRMW2_{jt} = \frac{DRNMW_{jt}}{(RAW_{jt})^2}$$

This variable used in conjunction with that in expression 25 allows for examination of impacts on average wages due to flows of workers that change the skill composition of employment in a region.

Coverage. Increased coverage of employment in other sectors could increase the effect of changes in the minimum wage on the average wage through the ripple effect or, with induced entry of other workers into the labor force, could alter the wage distribution. Flows of workers among industries of different types may not be the same, so that increased coverage of employment in some types of industries may have little relevance for others. This work distinguishes between coverage in other manufacturing industries and coverage in other private nonagricultural industries.

Let NNC_{it} be the national percentage of newly covered workers in year t who are subject to the federal minimum wage of $NNCMW_t$, and let NBC_{it} be the national percentage of previously covered workers in year t who are subject to the basic federal minimum wage, $NBMW_t$. A measure of coverage of employment in the ith industry by federal minimum-wage standards is

$$NCM_{it} = NBC_{it} + NNC_{it} \, (NNCMW_t/NBMW_t) \qquad (26)$$

which combines newly covered workers and previously covered workers, weighting the former by the ratio of the minimum wage applicable to newly covered workers to the basic federal minimum.

It is assumed that within an industry category, in the absence of state minimum-wage legislation, the national coverage measure,

NCM_{it}, is appropriate for measuring coverage in the jth SMSA. This abstracts from potential differences among SMSAs in the size composition of firms within an industry that would alter SMSA-specific employment coverage because of exemptions based on firm sales and other factors. The variation among SMSAs in the size composition of firms within an industry is less relevant than variation between SMSAs and less densely populated areas, however. Then, with $MW_{jt} = \text{Max}\,(NBMW_t, SMW_{jt})$, the larger of the state or federal minimum applicable to the jth SMSA, the percent of employment covered in the ith industry in the jth state is

$$TC_{ijt} = NCM_{it} + (1 - NCM_{it})(SMW_{jt}/MW_{jt}) \qquad (27)$$

which weights coverage under state legislation by the ratio of the state minimum to MW_{jt}. This weighting is similar to that used to combine NBC_{it} and NNC_{it} in determining NCM_{it}.[2]

Coverage in nonmanufacturing industries in the jth SMSA is given by

$$CO_{jt} = \sum (TC_{ijt} \cdot E_{ijt}) / E_{jt}$$

where i designates nonmanufacturing industry categories, E_{ijt} is employment in the ith manufacturing industry in region j, and E_{jt} is total employment in region j. This equation gives the percentage of covered employment in nonmanufacturing industries relative to total regional employment.

A similar measure for covered employment in other manufacturing industries is given by the share of other manufacturing employment in total employment in the jth SMSA, CM_{ijt}, which assumes complete coverage of all manufacturing industries. With CM_{jt} the ratio of covered manufacturing employment to total private nonagricultural employment in the jth SMSA and CO_{jt} the ratio of covered employment in other industries to total private nonagricultural employment in the jth SMSA, the variables used to capture impacts of coverage in other sectors on average wages are

$$DCOMW_{jt} = \frac{CO_{jt}RNMW_{jt} - CO_{jt-1}RNMW_{jt-1}}{RAW_{jt-1}RNMW_{jt-1}}$$

and

$$DCMMW_{jt} = \frac{CM_{jt}RNMW_{jt} - CM_{jt}RNMW_{jt-1}}{RAW_{jt-1}RNMW_{jt-1}}$$

[2] This measure is used when state legislation sets a single minimum wage as applicable to all employees. When the state minimum differs depending on industry, the relevant state minimum for the ith industry is used in expression 4.

84

If CO_{jt} and CM_{jt} are constant over time in a particular SMSA, percentage changes in the real national minimum wage are weighted by these shares. If CO_{jt} or CM_{jt} changes while $RNMW_{jt}$ is constant over time, the variables reduce to $(CO_{jt} - CO_{jt-1})/RAW_{jt}$ and $(CM_{jt} - CM_{jt-1})/RAW_{jt}$. For both cases the value is larger in low-cost-of-living areas because of deflation by RAW_{jt-1}.

Fluctuations in Economic Activity. General fluctuations in national economic activity are assumed here to be reflected by fluctuations in national output demand, taken as exogenous to each region. For industries producing for a national market, the relevant business cycle indicator is national. Variation in the demand for products affects the demand for labor, which leads to wage variation within an SMSA when the supply of labor is increasing in the short run. This modeling effort focuses on empirical specification of the nature of SMSA labor supply sensitivity to wage.

If workers flow among industries, a national output demand fluctuation in a particular industry, shifting demand for labor in that industry only, will affect wages only through the short-run labor supply of the whole SMSA. Hence the extent to which industry variation in labor demand affects wages will depend on the share of employment in that industry, relative to the rest of the SMSA, as well as on variation in labor demand in other manufacturing industries. Wage impacts in the ith industry in the jth SMSA due to fluctuations in national industrial production in the ith industry are captured by $S_{jt} DIP_{it}$, where S_{jt} is the share of the industry in total SMSA manufacturing employment and DIP_{it} is the percentage change in the national industrial production index for the ith industry. Effects from the rest of the SMSA are captured by $(1 - S_{jt}) DEOM_{jt}$, where $DEOM_{jt}$ is the percentage change in employment in other manufacturing industries in the jth SMSA.

To the extent that there are industry-specific or firm-specific skills for some or many workers, cyclical output demand patterns for one industry may not be affected by concurrent patterns in other industries. This suggests that use of actual S_{jt} is a lower bound for business cycle demand variations with the appropriate weighting of DIP_{it} and $DEOM_{jt}$, using S_{jt}^* where $S_{jt} < S_{jt}^* \leq 1$, the upper bound reflecting no interindustry movements of labor due to short-run fluctuations in output demand.

3. Econometric Specification and Empirical Results

Based on the discussion above of effects of various variables on the real average wage in a particular SMSA, equation 28 presents the

TABLE 9

POOLED CROSS SECTION OF TIME SERIES CLASSICAL LEAST SQUARES
ESTIMATES OF EQUATION 28, BY INDUSTRY
(time dummy variables not included)

Variable	Lumber and Wood Products [10]	Furniture and Fixtures [9]	Stone, Clay, and Glass Products [11]	Primary Metal Industries [19]	Fabricated Metal Industries [22]
DIP_t	.48	.58	1.66	.043	.042
	(.21)	(.33)	(.39)	(.065)	(.108)
DIP_{t-1}	−.004	−.38	−1.13	−.232	−.659
	(.018)	(.31)	(.40)	(.0078)	(.128)
DIP_{t-2}	−.005	.02	.17	−.014	.008
	(.021)	(.03)	(.07)	(.031)	(.027)
$DEOM_t$	.163	−.004	.31	.097	.062
	(.060)	(.051)	(.12)	(.040)	(.031)
$DEOM_{t-1}$	−.018	−.10	−.25	−.194	−.185
	(.023)	(.05)	(.14)	(.045)	(.038)
$DEOM_{t-2}$	.002	.02	.16	−.013	.007
	(.011)	(.03)	(.07)	(.027)	(.021)
DMW_t	.031	.026	.098	.008	.009
	(.024)	(.031)	(.071)	(.012)	(.011)
$D2MW_t$	.142	.083	.035	0.48	.031
	(.073)	(.081)	(.018)	(.027)	(.021)
$DCOMW_t$	−.042	−.021	−.071	−.009	−.003
	(.08)	(.16)	(.104)	(.006)	(.0027)
$DCMMW_t$	−.029	−.023	−.025	−.014	−.009
	(.03)	(.021)	(.031)	(.018)	(.007)
R^2	.32	.30	.28	.31	.30
F-statistic	2.31	2.03	2.09	3.13	3.17
deg. fre.	100	89	111	199	232

NOTE: SMSA dummy variables are included. Bracketed figures are the number of SMSAs in the sample. Figures in parentheses are standard errors.
SOURCE: Author.

estimated equation for a particular industry category. The term ($p + r_j$) is estimated using region-specific dummy variables, and $\phi(L)$ and $\theta(L)$, both polynomials in the lag operator, L, are assumed to be second-order. If ε_{jt} is independent and identically distributed for all (j,t), then classical least squares is an appropriate estimator, using the pooled cross section of time series. Moreover, with SMSA-specific

Machinery except Electrical [21]	Transportation Equipment [18]	Food and Kindred Products [22]	Apparel and Other Textile Products [18]	Printing and Publishing [21]	Chemicals and Petroleum [22]
0.89	.115	.002	.618	.010	−.051
(.071)	(.042)	(.171)	(.154)	(.228)	(.128)
−.281	−.173	.139	−.273	−.365	−.516
(.084)	(.046)	(.168)	(.180)	(.274)	(.137)
.032	−.053	−.035	.031	.025	.014
(.033)	(.036)	(.016)	(.024)	(.043)	(.041)
.029	.100	.043	.185	.091	.063
(.031)	(.043)	(.056)	(.038)	(.048)	(.034)
−.170	−.178	−.027	−.157	−.315	−.137
(.043)	(.046)	(.061)	(.045)	(.058)	(.040)
.012	−.053	−.023	.024	.043	.007
(.023)	(.033)	(.016)	(.026)	(.028)	(.025)
.015	.037	.009	0.21	.018	.056
(.033)	(.043)	(.011)	(.043)	(.027)	(.049)
.034	.013	.038	.106	.037	.118
(.021)	(.023)	(.027)	(.051)	(.020)	(.050)
−.014	−.0015	−.011	−.021	−.0000	−.014
(.009)	(.0023)	(.020)	(.017)	(.0005)	(.011)
−.006	.0009	−.047	−.012	−.0001	−.001
(.004)	(.0016)	(.021)	(.011)	(.0013)	(.001)
.26	.43	.26	.29	.34	.27
2.57	5.11	2.56	2.70	3.68	2.64
221	188	232	188	221	232

dummy variables, this relates to the fixed-effect model of Mundlak without a systematic time component.[3] Table 9 presents estimates of the parameters of expression 28 for each industrial category.[4]

[3] The estimation approach taken here involves using SMSA-specific dummy variables and year-specific dummy variables rather than an error component model. The implications of this approach are fully described in Yair Mundlak, "On the Pooling of Time Series and Cross Section Data," *Econometrica*, vol. 46, no. 1 (January 1978), pp. 69–85.

[4] Coefficients on the region-specific dummy variables that represent $(p + r_j)$ and coefficients on time dummy variables added in table 11 are not reported.

TABLE 10

Effects of Changes in Minimum Wages and Coverage on Average Real Wages, by Industry

(time-specific effects not included)

	Lumber and Wood Products	Furniture and Fixtures	Stone, Clay, and Glass Products	Primary Metal Industries
Percentage change in average real wage due to percentage change in the real national minimum wage	1.51 (0.71)	0.82 (0.49)	0.40 (0.23)	0.31 (0.24)
Percentage change in minimum wage effect due to change in $(1/RAW_{j,t-1})$, the regional deflator	0.92 (0.47)	0.54 (0.36)	0.30 (0.17)	0.25 (0.19)
Percentage change in real average wage due to change in coverage in other industries by one percent				
Nonmanufacturing coverage	−0.130 (0.26)	−0.065 (0.49)	−0.20 (0.30)	−0.023 (0.015)
Manufacturing coverage	−0.097 (0.098)	−0.071 (0.071)	−0.072 (0.089)	−0.036 (0.046)
Average coverage	−0.114 (0.061)	−0.068 (0.073)	−0.136 (0.107)	−0.030 (0.023)

NOTE: Figures in parentheses are standard errors.
SOURCE: Author; based on results in table 9.

$$DRAW_{jt} = p + r_j + \phi(L)S_{jt}DIP_t + \theta(L)(1 - S_{jt})DEOM_{jt}$$
$$+ \beta_1 DRMW_{jt} + \beta_2 DRMW2_{jt} + \beta_3 DCOMW_{jt}$$
$$+ \beta_4 DCMMW_{jt} + \varepsilon_{jt} \qquad (28)$$

The time series structure of ε_{jt} was examined independently for each SMSA. Durbin-Watson statistics (based on twelve observations) suggest no obvious first-order serial correlation of the errors. Estimates of the contemporaneous covariance matrix are available, although no statistical analysis was conducted regarding the off-diagonal elements. Standard errors of the estimates for each SMSA were similar, suggesting that no particular SMSA dominated the results or was extremely unexplained relative to the others.

Fabricated Metal Industries	Machinery, except Electrical	Transportation Equipment	Food and Kindred Products	Apparel and Textile Products	Printing and Publishing	Chemicals and Petroleum
0.25	0.25	0.16	0.29	1.62	0.26	0.98
(0.13)	(0.11)	(0.15)	(0.14)	(0.48)	(0.25)	(0.36)
0.18	0.19	0.10	0.22	0.84	0.20	0.68
(0.01)	(0.10)	(0.10)	(0.12)	(0.37)	(0.18)	(0.23)
−0.008	−0.037	−0.004	−0.031	−0.081	−0.000	−0.037
(0.007)	(0.024)	(0.006)	(0.056)	(0.066)	(0.001)	(0.029)
−0.025	−0.016	0.002	−0.132	−0.047	−0.002	−0.003
(0.019)	(0.011)	(0.0038)	(0.059)	(0.043)	(0.003)	(0.003)
−0.017	−0.027	−0.0007	−0.082	−0.064	−0.0001	0.020
(0.008)	(0.012)	(0.0012)	(0.043)	(0.038)	(0.0019)	(0.01)

Based on these results, table 10 shows effects of changes in the minimum wage and coverage on average hourly wages for each industry. The findings are indicative of three general results: (a) increases in the minimum wage induce increases in the average wage; (b) this increase is greater in otherwise lower-wage areas; and (c) increases in coverage of other sectors serve to decrease the average hourly wage.

The magnitude of the minimum-wage impact is often large, sometimes greater than unity in percentage terms. While estimates of increased coverage either in the rest of manufacturing or in non-manufacturing sectors are imprecise by themselves, their net impact is consistently negative and more precisely estimated. The coefficient

TABLE 11

POOLED CROSS SECTION OF TIME SERIES CLASSICAL LEAST SQUARES
ESTIMATES OF EQUATION 28, BY INDUSTRY
(time dummy variables included)

Variable	Lumber and Wood Products [10]	Furniture and Fixtures [9]	Stone, Clay, and Glass Products [11]	Primary Metal Industries [19]	Fabricated Metal Industries [22]
DIP_t	.29	−.14	1.80	.13	.033
	(.21)	(.40)	(.46)	(.08)	(.071)
DIP_{t-1}	.02	−.11	−1.10	.17	−.321
	(.02)	(.31)	(.48)	(.09)	(.160)
DIP_{t-2}	.02	.03	.17	−.01	−.015
	(.03)	(.03)	(.09)	(.03)	(.031)
$DECM_t$	.12	−.105	.36	.10	.018
	(.07)	(.07)	(.17)	(.06)	(.043)
$DEOM_{t-1}$	−.05	−.05	−.23	.04	−.053
	(.06)	(.07)	(.18)	(.06)	(.054)
$DEOM_{t-2}$	.02	.02	.17	−.004	−.014
	(.02)	(.03)	(.09)	(.025)	(.021)
DMW_t	.038	.021	.10	−.010	.014
	(.023)	(.022)	(.08)	(.031)	(.021)
$D2MW_t$	.162	.091	.033	.062	.034
	(.093)	(.131)	(.028)	(.131)	(.043)
$DCOMW_t$	−.102	−.031	−.043	−.0001	−.002
	(.046)	(.042)	(.061)	(.0006)	(.0017)
$DCMMW_t$	−.032	−.014	−.037	−.021	.022
	(.026)	(.004)	(.021)	(.014)	(.0046)
R^2	.38	.50	.31	.50	.38
F-statistic	1.66	2.52	1.39	4.65	3.21
deg. fre.	100	89	111	199	232

NOTE: SMSA and time dummy variables are included. Bracketed figures are the number of SMSAs in the sample. Figures in parentheses are standard errors.
SOURCE: Author.

on the variable intended to capture effects of flows of workers of different skills among regions is usually precisely estimated, suggesting that differences in cost of living among regions not only alter the initial impact of minimum wages on the wage distribution of workers but in addition lead to flows of lower-skill workers to high-cost-of-living areas and flows of higher-skill workers to low-cost-of-living regions.

Machinery except Electrical [21]	Transportation Equipment [18]	Food and Kindred Products [22]	Apparel and Other Textile Products [18]	Printing and Publishing [21]	Chemicals and Petroleum [22]
.094	.04	−.17	.13	−.37	−.10
(.101)	(.05)	(.16)	(.14)	(.22)	(.14)
.034	.08	.22	−.12	−.27	−.38
(.117)	(.07)	(.15)	(.13)	(.27)	(.14)
.002	−.04	−.04	.03	.005	.05
(.031)	(.041)	(.04)	(.02)	(.041)	(.04)
−.010	.04	−.13	−.05	−.06	.005
(.061)	(.06)	(.07)	(.05)	(.07)	(.052)
−.004	.07	.16	−.04	−.09	−.01
(.052)	(.06)	(.07)	(.05)	(.07)	(.05)
−.008	−.04	−.02	.01	.017	.02
(.021)	(.03)	(.01)	(.02)	(.028)	(.01)
.016	.041	.014	.026	.017	.040
(.031)	(.042)	(.017)	(.023)	(.021)	(.021)
0.48	.014	0.45	.097	.054	.135
(.031)	(.013)	(.031)	(.061)	(.031)	(.061)
−.021	−.0002	−.051	−.031	−.0002	−.037
(.013)	(.0003)	(.021)	(.014)	(.0005)	(.012)
−.011	.0008	.0002	−.009	.0001	.00001
(.006)	(.0013)	(.0007)	(.008)	(.0001)	(.0001)
.39	.58	.44	.55	.49	.37
3.17	6.14	4.03	5.51	4.85	3.06
221	188	221	177	210	221

Time-Specific Effects. Table 11 presents estimates of the parameters of equation 28 when time dummies are included in addition to the other variables. These are intended to capture year-specific, systematic components of average wage behavior in addition to region-specific components through SMSA dummy variables. While coefficients on DIP and $DEOM$ are affected by inclusion of year-specific effects, the coefficients associated with minimum-wage and coverage variables are not altered substantially. Table 12 shows estimated

TABLE 12

EFFECTS OF CHANGES IN MINIMUM WAGES AND COVERAGE ON
AVERAGE REAL WAGES, BY INDUSTRY
(time-specific effects included)

	Lumber and Wood Products	Furniture and Fixtures	Stone, Clay, and Glass Products	Primary Metal Industries
Percentage change in average real wage due to percentage change in the real national minimum wage	1.59 (0.64)	0.86 (0.42)	0.45 (0.21)	0.37 (0.26)
Percentage change in minimum wage effect due to change in $(1/RAW_{j,t-1})$, the regional deflator	1.09 (0.48)	0.58 (0.34)	0.29 (0.15)	0.30 (0.19)
Percentage change in real average wage due to change in coverage in other industries by 1 percent				
Nonmanufacturing coverage	−0.33 (0.15)	−0.095 (0.129)	−0.123 (0.175)	−0.00025 (0.0015)
Manufacturing coverage	−0.104 (0.084)	−0.043 (0.012)	−0.106 (0.060)	−0.053 (0.035)
Average coverage	−0.217 (0.086)	−0.069 (0.028)	−0.115 (0.091)	−0.027 (0.021)

SOURCE: Author. Based on results in table 11.

impacts of changes in the minimum wage and coverage based on results in table 11 and analogous to those in table 10.

Implications. These findings suggest that interindustry and regional flows of workers are a result of differences in coverage among industries and regional costs of living. Employment studies that aggregate over high- and low-wage regions capture only the net employment loss, possibly obscured by other factors. Effects of increased minimum wages on employment and compensation of workers depend on the extent of coverage, the empirical findings above indicating that simple indexes that combine coverage and minimum-wage levels into one measure are not appropriate for determining net employment impacts of minimum wages. Increased coverage in

Fabricated Metal Industries	Machinery, except Electrical	Transportation Equipment	Food and Kindred Products	Apparel and Other Textile Products	Printing and Publishing	Chemicals and Petroleum
0.29	0.34	0.18	0.31	1.48	0.36	0.99
(0.14)	(0.12)	(0.13)	(0.12)	(0.51)	(0.21)	(0.27)
0.20	0.27	0.11	0.27	0.78	0.28	0.76
(0.11)	(0.13)	(0.08)	(0.11)	(0.32)	(0.14)	(0.24)
−0.0055	−0.055	−0.0005	−0.143	−0.120	−0.00048	−0.098
(0.0047)	(0.034)	(0.0007)	(0.059)	(0.054)	(0.0012)	(0.032)
−0.0028	−0.029	0.0019	0.0006	−0.035	0.00024	0.00003
(0.0127)	(0.016)	(0.0031)	(0.0020)	(0.031)	(0.00024)	(0.00027)
−0.014	−0.042	0.0007	−0.071	−0.078	−0.00012	−0.049
(0.0010)	(0.017)	(0.0016)	(0.032)	(0.026)	(0.00021)	(0.014)

other sectors leads to a reduction in the average wage for previously covered sectors, suggesting that medium-skill workers enter the labor market because of increased market wages, replacing lower-skilled workers.

SELECTED AEI PUBLICATIONS

The AEI Economist, Herbert Stein, ed., published monthly (one year, $10; single copy, $1)

Changes in the Workweek of Fixed Capital: U.S. Manufacturing, 1929 to 1976, Murray F. Foss (104 pp., paper $5.25, cloth $12.25).

Minimum Wage Regulation in Retail Trade, Belton M. Fleisher (129 pp., paper $5.25, cloth $12.25)

Reindustrialization: Boon or Bane? John Charles Daly, mod. (31 pp., $3.75)

Wage Policy in the Federal Bureaucracy, George J. Borjas (59 pp., $4.25)

Minimum Wages, Fringe Benefits, and Working Conditions, Walter J. Wessels (97 pp., paper $4.25, cloth $11.25)

Poverty and the Minimum Wage, Donald O. Parsons (62 pp., $4.25)

The Constitution and the Budget, W.S. Moore and Rudolph G. Penner, eds. (172 pp., paper $6.25, cloth $14.25)

Value Added Taxation: The Experience of the United Kingdom, A.R. Prest (52 pp., $4.25)

Money and Liberty, S. Herbert Frankel (67 pp., $4.25)

International Liquidity Issues, Thomas D. Willett (114 pp., $5.25)

Prices subject to change without notice.

AEI ASSOCIATES PROGRAM

The American Enterprise Institute invites your participation in the competition of ideas through its AEI Associates Program. This program has two objectives:

The first is to broaden the distribution of AEI studies, conferences, forums, and reviews, and thereby to extend public familiarity with the issues. AEI Associates receive regular information on AEI research and programs, and they can order publications and cassettes at a savings.

The second objective is to increase the research activity of the American Enterprise Institute and the dissemination of its published materials to policy makers, the academic community, journalists, and others who help shape public attitudes. Your contribution, which in most cases is partly tax deductible, will help ensure that decision makers have the benefit of scholarly research on the practical options to be considered before programs are formulated. The issues studied by AEI include:

- Defense Policy
- Economic Policy
- Energy Policy
- Foreign Policy
- Government Regulation
- Health Policy
- Legal Policy
- Political and Social Processes
- Social Security and Retirement Policy
- Tax Policy

For more information, write to:

AMERICAN ENTERPRISE INSTITUTE
1150 Seventeenth Street, N.W.
Washington, D.C. 20036